New Orleans, Louisiana

2025 to 2026

Fun Activities, Must do's and Hidden Gems

JourneyJoy Journeys

All rights reserved.

No part of this publication may be reproduced, distributed, or transmitted in any form or by any means, including photocopying, recording, or other electronic or mechanical methods, without the prior written permission of the publisher, except in the case of brief quotations embodied in critical reviews and certain other noncommercial uses permitted by copyright law.

Copyright © JourneyJoy Journeys, 2024.

This guidebook is meant to help visitors learn about New Orleans's beautiful past, lively culture, delicious food, and soulful music. The guide comes with insider tips, creative ideas, information on both famous and lesser known gems, and carefully chosen activities. With ideas for unique events, trips that are good for families, affordable tours, and love getaways. Go in, look around, and let this magical city amaze you.

CONTENTS

THE CRESCENT CITY — 6
A City of Soul: Music, Food, and Culture — 6
Weather and Packing Ideas — 11
Budget friendly Accommodation Options — 14

MUST SEE ATTRACTIONS — 20
The Soul of New Orleans: History and Heritage — 34
Outdoor Activities and Adventures — 47
Family-Friendly Activities — 53

A CULINARY JOURNEY THROUGH NEW ORLEANS — 60
Sweet Delights & Recipes to Sample — 60
Top Eats and Restaurants — 63

JAZZ & LIVE MUSIC EXPERIENCES — 74

HIDDEN GEMS AND OFF-THE-BEATEN-PATH ACTIVITIES — 88

SHOPPING AND SOUVENIRS — 105

SEASONAL ACTIVITIES AND CELEBRATIONS — 109

   Spring: Blooms, Music, and Outdoor Fun — 109

   Summer: Beating the Heat with Indoor Escapes — 114

   Fall: Halloween Parades and Haunted Tours — 124

   Winter: Christmas and New Year's Fireworks — 129

ESSENTIAL TIPS FOR TRAVELERS — 134

   Navigating New Orleans' Public Transportation — 134

   Important Emergency Contacts and Information — 138

   Apps and Websites to Make Your Stay Smoother — 140

FINAL WORDS — 142

THE CRESCENT CITY

A City of Soul: Music, Food, and Culture

The soulful fusion of music, cuisine, and culture that permeates every street, every corner, and every conversation is what makes New Orleans a special place. This city encourages you to experience life with excitement, passion, and authenticity, with tastes as vibrant as the colors of a Mardi Gras float and a rhythm as steady as a jazz beat. Jazz is said to have originated in New Orleans, but the city's music is also a means of expressing one's identity and sense of community.

You can hear it wherever you go: gospel singers uplifting the spirits in nearby churches, blues gushing from bars in the French Quarter, and soulful brass bands parading in the Treme. A diverse range of cultures, including French folk songs, Caribbean beats, and African rhythms, gave rise to the city's distinctive musical traditions. New Orleans became a worldwide music hub as a result of the emergence of legendary artists like Louis

Armstrong, Sidney Bechet, and Jelly Roll Morton. Jazz is just the start, however; the city's musical heritage also includes funk, R&B, zydeco, and bounce music. Known as the "local's Bourbon Street,Frenchmen Street is home to some of the greatest live music venues, with weekly concerts held at small venues including The Spotted Cat and d.b.a. Buskers transform ordinary moments into concerts by performing passionately on street corners that also serve as stages.

Then comes the second line, an impromptu procession that seems like unadulterated happiness in action. These festivities representing life, death, and rebirth and are led by a brass band, originated from African American funeral processions. These days, second lines serve as a gathering place for weddings, anniversaries, or just because, in New Orleans, it's always the perfect moment to celebrate. In New Orleans, food is also a narrative, an art form, and an experience. The city's food is a reflection of its many cultural influences; it combines tastes from French, Spanish, African, and Creole cooking to create meals that fulfill the senses and tantalize the eyes. Start your morning with a chicory-infused café au lait and some hot, fluffy doughnuts drenched in powdered sugar, known as beignets from Café du Monde. A po'boy sandwich, which is a crusty French bread packed with roast beef, fried shrimp, or oysters and dripping with gravy or spicy sauce, is a must-have for lunch. A trip to New Orleans wouldn't be complete without sampling gumbo, a filling stew with West African culinary roots that is often made with okra, sausage, and shrimp stewed in a thick roux.

Here, Cajun and Creole cuisines are featured equally. While Cajun cuisine; think boudin sausage and blackened fish, comes from the Acadians who lived in rural Louisiana, Creole cuisine, such as jambalaya and crawfish bisque, reflects the impact of French colonizers and African customs. The food of New Orleans is known for its rich tastes, robust spices, and large amounts, since providing nutritious food to someone is considered a gesture of love. And then there are, of course, festivals that celebrate food. Adding to world-class concerts, the New Orleans Jazz & Heritage Festival offers a variety of food, including pralines and crawfish bread. The city's favorite sandwich is served in imaginative ways during the annual Po-Boy Festival, demonstrating how innovative and deeply ingrained New Orleans cuisine is.

New Orleans culture is distinct from other cultures, combining holy customs and inventive modernism with an air of old-world charm. A spirit of togetherness and celebration where life is lived boldly, unabashedly, and with tremendous delight is at the core of this blending of cultures. The most well-known manifestation of the city's cultural character is "Mardi Gras." It's a season that starts on Twelfth Night and reaches its peak on Fat Tuesday.

Along the parade route, Mardi Gras krewes toss beads, cash, and trinkets to attendees while organizing intricate floats and masked balls. This is also a festival that unites generations and is a family custom. The city's joyful mood endures throughout the year with smaller parades and street festivities, even if you miss Mardi Gras. The respect for spirituality is another essential component of New Orleans culture. The city's strong ties to voodoo and Catholicism illustrate how European and African traditions have blended. Voodoo stores and shrines are scattered throughout the French Quarter, giving insight into a custom that respects ancestors and the force of nature.

Fundamentally, New Orleans is a city of strong, innovative, and very hospitable people. With grace, humor, and an unyielding confidence in the value of joy, the people of New Orleans bear the burden of history and adversity. The culture is lived here on the streets, in talks with people, in a shared meal at a local restaurant, or in the rhythm of a drum at a second line; it is not limited to museums or monuments. You learn to slow down, enjoy the present, and engage with the environment around you.

Weather and Packing Ideas

The majority of the year is warm in New Orleans' with humid subtropical climate characterized by fluctuating humidity levels and occasional downpours.

- The weather throughout the spring season (March to May) is mild and pleasant, with highs in the 70s to 80s°F (21 to 29°C) which means there will be occasional rains. Pack light layers, like a rain jacket, a light sweater, and T-shirts. For outdoor events, comfortable footwear is essential.

- The summer months of June through August are characterized by hot, muggy, and often wet weather, with highs around 90°F (32-37°C) with thunderstorms occurring often. Bring breathable, light clothes (like linen or cotton), a hat, sunscreen, an umbrella, and a rain poncho. Sunglasses and sandals are also smart choices. Do not forget to drink plenty of water.

- The weather during the fall season (September to November) is warm and less humid, with highs in the 70s to 80s°F (21 to 29°C) with sporadic rainfall, particularly from June to November when hurricanes are active. Short sleeves throughout the day and a jumper or jacket for chilly nights are the ideal light layers. You still need a little umbrella.

- The weather is mild with sporadic cold fronts throughout the winter months of December through February. The range of temperatures is 40-60°F (4-18°C). Snow is uncommon, although rain is probable. Pack a variety of layers, including cozy leggings, a light jacket or sweater, and long-sleeve shirts. If a cold front arrives, you might need a warmer coat.

The best way to see New Orleans is on foot; therefore, it is imperative that you wear shoes that are comfortable for walking.

Keep a small umbrella or rain jacket with you at all times since unexpected downpours are often. Bug spray is beneficial, particularly when mosquitoes are active during the warmer months and a reusable water bottle is essential for staying hydrated, more so during hot weather.

Budget friendly Accommodation Options

- **India House Hostel**

With nightly prices running from $50, India House Hostel provides a lively and reasonably priced stay. The bohemian-style hostel is housed at 124 S Lopez St, New Orleans, LA 70119, in a quaint Victorian house in a quiet residential neighborhood. It is conveniently close to the city's major attractions, being just a 2-minute walk from the Canal and Salcedo streetcar station. It is a wonderful starting point for exploration since the renowned French Quarter is only three miles away.

The hostel offers a variety of basic lodging options, such as coed and single-sex dormitories with free Wi-Fi and bunk beds. Public restrooms are available while private rooms can accommodate up to two people and some have en suite bathrooms. The facilities of India House offer a relaxed, friendly environment. There is a common kitchen, a cozy TV area, and a courtyard with a swimming pool, picnic tables, BBQ grills, and even a stage for live music performances. With an inexpensive three-day Jazzy Pass that grants unlimited trips, the streetcar station just outside makes it simple to explore the city.

- **HI New Orleans Hostel**

Starting at $25 per night, HI New Orleans Hostel gives its guests a remarkable combination of price and comfort. The hostel is conveniently located at *1028 Canal St, New Orleans, LA 70112,* across from a streetcar station, making it simple to go about the city. Visitors can explore the famous St. Louis Cathedral, a mile distant, or take in the vibrant ambiance of Bourbon Street, which is just a 14-minute walk away. Convenience is increased by the nearby cafés, stores, and convenient transit alternatives. The accommodations include both mixed-gender and single-sex dormitories with thoughtful features like private outlets, reading lamps, and bunk beds with privacy curtains. There are common restrooms and lockers available. The hostel also has chic private rooms with private bathrooms. Visitors can chat in the large common space with a pool table and a colorful painting, unwind in the café with a terrace, or use the fully furnished communal kitchen. To begin the day, a continental breakfast is also offered. With extra amenities like safe baggage storage, laundry rooms, and quick access to transit.

- **The Quisby**

Starting at $84 a night, the Quisby provides a cozy and reasonably priced stay. It is a laid-back hostel conveniently located at 1225 St Charles Ave, New Orleans, LA 70130, close to a streetcar stop in the Lower Garden District, making it simple to explore the city. The French Quarter's Jackson Square is about two miles distant, which increases its allure for visitors wishing to remain near important landmarks. Both female-only and mixed-gender dormitories with private lockers, en suite bathrooms, reading-light

16

bunk beds, and Wi-Fi are available for groups of four to six individuals. There are also private rooms with cozy mattresses, TVs with streaming capabilities, and contemporary bathrooms with walk-in showers for more seclusion. A refrigerator and additional storage space are included in some rooms. The lobby's wood-paneled dining room, which also has a welcoming bar, is where guests can have breakfast. Bike storage, washing facilities, and access to communal kitchen appliances like a refrigerator and microwave are extra features.

- **Madame Isabelle's House In New Orleans**

Tucked at *1021 Kerlerec St, New Orleans, LA 70116*, on a quiet residential street, Madame Isabelle's House is a historic, vividly decorated residence that makes for a warm and inviting stay. This laid-back hostel is a wonderful choice for comfort and camaraderie without going over budget, with nightly prices beginning at $26. Its ideal location puts visitors within easy walking distance of Bourbon Street's lively nightlife (12 minutes),

Jackson Square (17 minutes), and I-10. Accommodations include female-only and mixed-gender dormitories with free Wi-Fi, communal toilets, and bunk beds. There are unique private rooms that can accommodate up to three people and have either shared or en suite amenities for more solitude. In addition to using a shared kitchen, visitors can have breakfast every morning in a classy dining area. The hostel's quaint lounge and garden terrace that includes a hot tub, are ideal places to relax. Meeting other tourists is made simple by frequent excursions and activities that promote a feeling of community.

- **Auberge NOLA Hostel**

With nightly prices from $15, Auberge NOLA Hostel offers a warm and reasonably priced stay with quick access to New Orleans' main attractions and is situated at *1628 Carondelet St, New Orleans, LA 70130*, one block from the St. Charles at Euterpe Streetcar Station. The hostel is an excellent starting point for visiting the city since it is less than a mile from the Greyhound bus terminal and just two miles from the busy Bourbon Street. Air-conditioned dormitories with bedding, towels, and lockers for up to eight people are available for both mixed and female-only visitors. For the convenience of visitors,  communal single-sex restrooms are maintained tidy. Bunk beds, kitchen, and living room are included in a bright apartment with its own entrance for a more private stay. The option that accepts visitors 40 years of age and over, is perfect for those who want more solitude without sacrificing the hostel's sense of community. Great places to relax and mingle include the hostel's courtyard and light-filled sunroom, furnished with board games and Wi-Fi. Solo travelers will be made to feel extra welcome by the welcoming staff, who are available to give suggestions and plan group activities.

MUST SEE ATTRACTIONS

New Orleans is a city bursting with vibrant culture, rich history, and unforgettable experiences. Comprising lively streets filled with jazz, tranquil parks and historic landmarks, there's something to captivate every visitor. And whatever it is you're drawn to, be it the music, architecture, or local flavors, these attractions present a perfect introduction to the spirit of the Crescent City.

- **French Quarter Visitor Center**

The National Park Service's French Quarter Visitor Center at 419 Decatur St, New Orleans, LA 70130, presents an enthralling look into New Orleans's diverse history and culture. This free-entry center at the core of the French Quarter, is an excellent place to start exploring the rich history of the city. Inside, fascinating displays explore subjects including jazz's origins, Creole customs, and the long-lasting effects of segregation and slavery on the music and culture of the area. In addition to offering historical insights, rangers offer guided walking tours and give advice on the best places to eat, drink, and engage in family-friendly activities in the area. The ranger lecture, focusing on the city's musical development via the prism of historical conflicts and cultural fusion, is a fan favorite and starts at 10 AM. It vividly depicts the unique rhythms of New Orleans and how they were influenced by a variety of sources via in-depth narrative. Visitors should plan early, as these participatory seminars regularly attract a throng.

Beyond the displays, the center's outdoor courtyard with bathrooms, blooming flowers, and shaded trees, provides a tranquil haven from the busy streets. It's the ideal spot to unwind before or after seeing the Quarter. Plus, the center offers free live jazz concerts that evoke the essence of New Orleans and provide guests with a memorable experience. Books and mementos that capture the essence of the city are available at a tiny and well-chosen gift store. Families will also benefit from the Junior Ranger program that connects kids to local history and neighboring sites like the Jazz

Museum via interactive activities. The tourist center is open every day from 9:30 AM to 4:30 PM (save from Sundays and Mondays), and creates a warm setting for learning, relaxing, and taking in the spirit of New Orleans.

- **Bourbon Street**

An exciting encounter that really embodies New Orleans' spirit may be had on Bourbon Street. This iconic boulevard located at *Bourbon St, New Orleans, LA 70112*, is open twenty-four hours a day, and is always bustling with activity. Bourbon Street is a bustling mix of bars, restaurants, and small businesses that welcome guests to experience the finest of New Orleans culture. It is well-known for its colorful architecture, elaborate balconies, and energetic people. With jazz, blues, and rock erupting from venues onto the streets and generating an irresistible energy that keeps patrons dancing from bar to bar, the music scene is unparalleled. The air is charged with excitement during parades, particularly around Mardi Gras, when it's almost a sport to grab beads thrown from floats. From boutique stores to quaint cafés, the side lanes that branch off Bourbon offer even more hidden treasures. Beyond the celebration and music, Bourbon Street serves delicious cuisine that captures the distinct tastes of New Orleans. It's simple to get started with the local Creole and Cajun food at the restaurants that line the street, serving classic meals like gumbo, jambalaya, and fresh beignets. One of the street's most spectacular events, Mardi Gras, turns Bourbon Street into a glittering festival complete with colorful costumes, enormous parades, and joyful beads. The street is perfect for experiencing the city's nightlife since, while it becomes more family-friendly during the day, it takes on a wild, party-filled vibe at night.

- **St. Louis Cathedral**

One of New Orleans' most recognizable structures, St. Louis Cathedral offers a unique combination of spirituality, beauty, and history. Crowned by its characteristic triple spires, the cathedral was first completed in 1718 and rebuilt in 1789 after terrible fires under Spanish control, and exhibits an exquisite fusion of French and Spanish architectural forms. The church lies at *615 Pere Antoine Alley, New Orleans, LA 70116*, in the center of Jackson Square, and is a popular destination because of its majesty and serene ambiance. The inside of the cathedral, which is open daily from 9 a.m. to 4 p.m., has exquisite stained-glass windows, elaborately painted ceilings, and peaceful candle lit areas ideal for introspection. Even for those who are not religious, the intricate paintings that cover the chapel ceilings are a highlight and make the visit worthwhile. Visitors can purchase affordable Catholic souvenirs from a tiny on-site gift store, enabling them to carry a memento of the event home.

Adding to its religious importance, the cathedral actively participates in New Orleans' cultural life. Events like baptisms or daily masses, giving an insight into the spiritual customs of the local community can be explored by visitors. The cathedral's location in Jackson Square, surrounded by vibrant artists and street entertainers as well as neighborhood eateries serving French Quarter cuisine, further to its allure. The plaza itself provides a vibrant contrast after a quiet spell inside, and visitors will find distinctive eateries and stores around. Even though the neighborhood might be busy, it adds to the city's personality and the lively spirit that makes New Orleans so special.

- **Audubon Park**

Audubon Park is a large urban sanctuary ideal for leisure, entertainment, and outdoor activities. It is situated at *6500 Magazine St, New Orleans, LA 70118,* in the historic Uptown area. The park is open every day from 5 a.m. to 10 p.m., and offers a serene environment for leisurely walks, lakes brimming with birds, and century-old oak trees covered in Spanish moss. The park is surrounded by a paved 1.8-mile bike and jogging path well-marked for bikers and pedestrians and has cool spots perfect for cooling down in the summer. The park is ideal for family get-togethers, business parties, and

25

gatherings since it has three playgrounds, beautiful picnic spaces along the river, and picnic shelters that can be rented. Any visit is made more interesting by the availability of tennis courts, horseback riding opportunities, and outdoor exercise stations for keeping active.

There is an 18-hole competitive golf course in the park, and the well-kept walkways give simple access to tranquil lagoons and picturesque views of the affluent residences that line the park's edge. The park serves both residents and visitors tranquil outdoor experiences with free parking, spotless facilities, and roomy comfy seats. There are more activities offered at the nearby zoo, Audubon Park. The park invites visitors time and time again since it provides a revitalizing respite from the bustle of the city.

- **The National WWII Museum**

Stories of courage, sacrifice, and international battle are brought to life at the National WWII Museum giving an immersive trip through one of history's most significant eras. With displays spanning both the European and Pacific theaters of the war, the multi-building complex, which is open daily from 9 a.m. to 5 p.m., offers a profoundly immersive experience. The museum gives visitors a close-up look at the lives of soldiers, airmen, and civilians by skillfully balancing historical data with first-person accounts. Every visitor will be enthralled by the extensive galleries, interactive submarine exhibit, and real WWII aircraft on display. The 4-D theater that uses strong audiovisual effects to bring important moments to life, significantly improves the experience.

Tickets start at $32, with senior, student, child, and veteran discounts available. The museum's structure allows for self-paced exploration. It's simple to spend many hours at the museum and yet feel like there's more to see because of the variety of material. To fully understand the richness of the displays, visitors should schedule a full day or perhaps space out their visit across many trips. To provide comprehensive knowledge of the war, the museum makes sure to cover all of the main fronts, including the less well-known Pacific campaign. In order to enable visitors to rest in between galleries, there is also a restaurant on the premises. The museum is a must-visit for history buffs wishing to comprehend the sacrifices that molded the contemporary world since it is conveniently located near the French Quarter.

- **New Orleans Museum of Art**

Over 40,000 pieces from various historical eras and international creative styles can be explored at the New Orleans Museum of Art (NOMA). The museum is housed at *1 Collins Diboll Cir, New Orleans, LA 70124,* in a magnificent marble edifice, and presente a wide range of art; modern, Japanese, African as well as traditional European paintings. Visitors can easily spend hours perusing its exquisitely selected galleries that include exhibitions on three levels. Admission to the museum starts from $20 per person, with military members receiving a discount and minors under certain circumstances entering free of charge. NOMA is a wonderful place to spend a weekend or an inside activity on wet days since it is open every day except Mondays. There is a lot of walking to see the whole collection of art on show, so comfortable shoes are advised. The nearby Sydney and Walda Besthoff Sculpture Garden, a free outdoor area with more than 90 sculptures tucked away amid tranquil surroundings, is one of the museum's attractions. In the park that surrounds the museum, visitors can also explore Big Lake, where renting a paddle boat adds an additional element of excitement. During a visit, the museum café is a tranquil place to have coffee or a meal while taking in views of the surrounding lakes and sculpture garden. NOMA is a wonderful place for both art lovers and casual tourists because of its well-considered blend of indoor and outdoor events.

- **Shops of the Colonnade**

Located at *1008 N Peters St, New Orleans, LA 70116*, the Shops of the Colonnade offers a vibrant and varied shopping experience and is a vintage marketplace open every day from 10 AM to 6 PM, with a range of regional merchants selling apparel and handcrafted goods, gifts and souvenirs. With vendors serving both classic New Orleans cuisines and unusual goodies like beignets, jambalaya, and even crepes, foodies will have no shortage of meals to enjoy. Exploring the city's culture via its craftsmen and gastronomic pleasures is made possible by the lively environment that is teeming with energy and the sounds of local conversation.

The allure of an outdoor bazaar, where every seller contributes something unique, is there while strolling around the market. While taking in the relaxed atmosphere of the region, visitors can purchase fresh vegetables, Mardi Gras-themed souvenirs, and tiny trinkets to take home. Conveniently situated next to Jackson Square, it's simple to spend a few hours perusing, dining, and taking in the vibrant atmosphere. The market's variety of goods and friendly traders make it worth visiting, even if it's busy.

- **Mardi Gras World**

An immersive behind-the-scenes look into the colorful world of New Orleans' most well-known celebration is provided by Mardi Gras World. The beauty of Mardi Gras floats is brought to life at this expansive 400,000-square-foot facility, open every day from 9 AM to 5:30 PM. Visitors will experience the beauty and workmanship behind the stunning parade floats, with admission prices beginning at $21 per person.

Every hour, for forty to fifty minutes, guided tours give intriguing insights into the complex process of creating floats, from conception to completion. The experience is made sweeter by the opportunity for guests to eat a piece of classic King Cake along the route. With hundreds of colorful sets, costumes, and sculptures to see, the complex gives plenty of opportunity to explore outside of the guided tour. Visitors will see creation in action, as artists often work on future projects on site. The area is ideal for taking pictures because of its vibrant and vivid exhibits. Although there are free shuttle services, it's best to verify the schedule and make a pickup call in advance.

- **Steamboat NATCHEZ - Official Site**

Along the Mississippi River, the Steamboat NATCHEZ sets up a nostalgic voyage that combines food, music, and history to create an experience that will never be forgotten. Every day from 8 AM to 7 PM, two-hour cruises are offered, with tickets starting at $42 per person. During a guided engine room tour, visitors will get a personal look at the genuine paddlewheel mechanisms of the last steam-powered boat on the river.

With live narration that shares insights into New Orleans' rich history and present, the voyage, taken either during the day or at night, gives stunning views of the busy port and the surrounding city. Traditional jazz music is available to passengers on board; during day cruises, a trio performs, and at night, a complete five-piece band entertains the guests. Buffet-style meals with Southern staples like gumbo are available for dining, and brunch cruises give an additional layer of decadence. Both alcoholic and non-alcoholic drinks are available for purchase in the bars located on each deck. The top deck's shade makes it the ideal place to unwind and enjoy the river air.

The Soul of New Orleans: History and Heritage

The soul of New Orleans is deeply rooted in its rich history and vibrant heritage, a blend of French, Spanish, Creole, and African influences. This city tells its story through music, architecture, cuisine, and traditions, with each neighborhood giving a glimpse into the past. Through historic landmarks and cultural institutions, New Orleans invites visitors to explore the events, people, and artistry that have shaped its unique identity over centuries.

- **St. Louis Cemetery No. 1 Official Tour**

An immersive experience through the most famous cemetery in New Orleans, where tradition, culture, and history all coexist, is provided by the Official Tour of St. Louis Cemetery No. 1. It has above-ground graves, a characteristic derived from the city's distinctive burial practices, and is one of the oldest cemeteries in the city. Through this guided tour, guests can go behind the iron gates and see the last resting places of famous people like civil rights activist Homer Plessy and Voodoo priestess Marie Laveau. Beginning at the Basin St.  Station Visitor Center, the trip presents an unforgettable glimpse into the essence of the city by covering fascinating information about the people, tales, and customs that built New Orleans. With admission priced at $25 per person and open every day from 9 a.m. to 4 p.m., visitors should keep in mind to purchase tickets in advance.

The 45-minute tour gives guests a close-up look at the art, culture, and customs surrounding New Orleans' burial traditions while striking a balance between history and narrative. Visitors should remember to remain hydrated throughout the trip. Additional conveniences include air conditioning, bathrooms, and a cold drink and gift store at the Basin St. Station Visitor Center. Even though the trip covers a lot of ground in a short amount of time, the small group sizes guarantee a customized experience, enabling visitors to interact with the complex history behind each tomb and ask questions.

- **Gallier House**

A fascinating look into the mid-19th century lifestyle of a prosperous New Orleans family can be experienced at Gallier House. This well-preserved Victorian mansion at *1132 Royal St, New Orleans, LA 70116*, was constructed in 1861 by famous architect James Gallier Jr., and exemplifies the inventiveness and genius of its era. The home has unusual features for the time, including an experimental skylight, hot and cold running water, and a peaceful courtyard covered in flora, in addition to its elaborate interiors and period furniture.

A somber reminder of the enslaved individuals who lived in houses like these in the French Quarter are the adjacent slave quarters, which are also accessible to visitors. The museum is open every day except Tuesdays from 9:30 a.m. to 3:30 p.m., and admission prices start at $18 per person. The tour explores the social issues of the era, including the Gallier family's customs and the part slaves played in sustaining such luxurious lives, adding to giving an architectural tour. Every room has been carefully chosen to recreate the essence of the Victorian period; some tours even concentrate on certain subjects, such as funeral customs and burial rites. While the house's historical authenticity guarantees a profound and thought-provoking experience, the beautiful courtyard lends a peaceful touch to the visit. The Gallier House is sometimes combined with the neighboring Hermann-Grima House for visitors who want to learn more, giving a more comprehensive view of upper-class life in New Orleans.

- **New Orleans Pharmacy Museum**

Located at *514 Chartres St, New Orleans, LA 70130,* in a quaint 1823 drugstore in the French Quarter, the New Orleans Pharmacy Museum gives a unique exploration of the city's medical history. This museum displays the evolution of healthcare over centuries with its extensive collection of ancient medical tools, old apothecary jars, and early medicinal artifacts. The displays give an insight into the advancement of science as well as the odd behaviors that influenced early medicine in New

Orleans, ranging from herbal medicines to superstition cures. Visitors can tour two levels full of well-kept relics, such as early pharmaceutical machinery, soda fountains, and optometry equipment. The museum is open every day from 10 a.m. to 4 p.m., although closed on Sundays and Mondays. Admission is $10 per person. This museum provides an engaging visit, both through a guided experience for deeper insights or a self-guided tour at your leisure.

Guests can follow the history of medicine because of the well-planned exhibits and thorough labeling that vividly tell the tale of each item. Old prescriptions, medical equipment, and pharmacy records on the upper level display intriguing oddities, including historically infamously bad handwriting. The museum offers a nostalgic and instructive experience with its finely preserved cabinets and historical charm.

- **Congo Square**

Congo Square offers a distinctive fusion of history, culture, peace and quiet. It is situated at *701 N Rampart St, New Orleans, LA 70116,* in Louis Armstrong Park in the historic Tremé area. Through song, dance, and rituals, it evolved from a crucial meeting spot for enslaved people to a significant component of African cultural expression. This open area is still bustling with activity today, holding festivals, drum circles, and concerts, all of which help maintain the creative and communal atmosphere.

Open every day from 8 a.m. to 7 p.m., Congo Square is a wonderful place to have a picnic or take a leisurely stroll. The region is renowned for its sculptures, lovely walkways, placid ponds, and expansive trees, one of which is an old family tree that silently bears witness to many generations of tales. In order to strengthen the bond with those who came before them, visitors often make gifts. The custom of drum circles that has been practiced for more than 300 years, comes to life on Sundays from 3 to 6 p.m., when the air is filled with strong beats. Plus providing a respite from the bustling streets of the French Quarter, strolling around the plaza allows one to consider the cultural importance ingrained in the area. To really appreciate the park's significance, it's important to visit with some previous knowledge or take a guided tour, even though the sculptures and picturesque vistas inspire a link to history.

- **Hermann-Grima House**

Through its period furniture and elegant architecture, the Hermann-Grima House, a wonderfully restored 19th-century residence at *820 St Louis St, New Orleans, LA 70112,* in the French Quarter, encourages guests to discover New Orleans' complex past. The 1831-built home's Federalist façade, original open-hearth kitchen, and large courtyard provide a window into the way of life of the city's wealthy elite. The Urban Enslavement Tour, which explores the lives of individuals enslaved in an urban setting, is one of the experience's highlights. This fascinating tour highlights the significant contributions of persons of African origin to the cultural and historical fabric of New Orleans by illuminating how their experiences varied from those who were enslaved in rural regions. The tour is a must-see for interests comprehending the nuances of New Orleans history. The Hermann-Grima House is open every day from 10 a.m. to 4 p.m. (closed on Tuesdays) and provides an interesting and thought-provoking educational experience. Visitors may explore the main house furnished with real items that vividly depict the past, and see the well-preserved slave quarters standing in stark contrast to the lavish interior. Plus the tours, the site has a carriage house from the 19th century home to The Exchange Shop, a notable nonprofit organization run by women and established in 1881, demonstrating the continuous tradition of women's achievements in the South.

- **BK Historic House and Gardens**

Founded in 1826 as a National Historic Landmark, the BK Historic House and Gardens allows guests to go back in time and learn about the lives of notable New Orleans residents from the 19th century. A magnificent example of the raised cottage architecture, this gorgeous home was renovated by

famed novelist Frances Parkinson Keyes in 1948 and exhibits a distinctive fusion of Creole and American architectural elements. Entry costs are from $11 per person, and visitors can take guided tours that highlight the rich history housed inside. With its elaborate ironwork, gas-lit chandeliers, and exquisitely designed furniture, the mansion has mostly been preserved, giving visitors a personal look at how wealthy people in New Orleans used to live.

The BK House is open every day from 10 a.m. to 3 p.m. (closed on Sundays) and presents an interesting tour of its charming grounds and well-preserved rooms. The informed guides weave together tales that vary from the tragic to the inspirational, offering engrossing insights into the lives of the families that called this place home. Plus, visitors may take in the tranquil garden that acts as a tranquil haven in the middle of the busy city, and the collection of antique dolls displaying the artistry of a bygone period. Special activities, like concerts in the garden, add to the experience and provide a lovely fusion of history and culture.

- **Chalmette Battlefield and National Cemetery**

Visitors can take a trip back in time to Chalmette Battlefield and National Cemetery, where they can experience the crucial moments of the War of 1812. It serves as the backdrop for the Battle of New Orleans, showcasing the tactics and victories that made Andrew Jackson a household name. With signs outlining significant events of the fight and their importance. Exhibits and relics in the visitor center bring history to life, while captivating film presentations give a better understanding of the conflict. Questions will be answered by knowledgeable park rangers, enhancing the experience. A tiny gift store sells books and souvenirs, and admission is free. Though summer visitors should expect the heat, the battlefield offers a wonderful opportunity for introspection.

43

The Chalmette National Cemetery, a magnificent location that pays tribute to those who fought for many generations, is just beyond the battlefield. Reflecting the sacrifice of more than 15,000 Americans, including soldiers from every significant combat between the War of 1812 and the Vietnam War, the cemetery is lined with neat graves and runs along a small road. A soldier who participated in the actual fight celebrated at Chalmette is buried among the dead. It is one of the most unique national cemeteries in the United States because of the serene surroundings that encourage introspection. Visitors should stroll around this melancholy area and absorb the history and tales it contains. The facility provides a meaningful and reflective experience, combining historical education with peaceful and reflective times, thanks to its beautiful gardens and thought-provoking exhibitions.

- **Backstreet Cultural Museum**

With an emphasis on the colorful worlds of brass bands, jazz funerals, second-line parades, and the Mardi Gras Indians, the Backstreet Cultural Museum sets up an enthralling look into New

Orleans' distinctive customs. The museum, housed  at *1531 St Philip St, New Orleans, LA 70116*, in the historic Treme district that is known as the oldest African-American community in the United States, is brimming with elaborate beading, stunning costumes, and mementos that showcase years of cultural expression. With costumes created by locals, each display highlights the talent and commitment of regional designers. To establish a meaningful link between historical struggles and current festivities, visitors will learn about the history of the Mardi Gras Indians, who trace their beginnings to African-American and Native American partnerships.

With each piece and exhibit telling a narrative, the museum offers a rich, immersive experience ideal for introducing visitors to the customs that characterize New Orleans. A greater comprehension of the cultural relevance of Carnival festivities, jazz funerals, and second lines can be gained via the museum's guided tours. In-depth accounts of the development of these traditions and their significance to the local community are shared by knowledgeable guides, many of whom have personal ties to the traditions. The late Sylvester Francis founded the collection, which has now expanded into a remarkable archive that provides visitors with a glimpse of the city's vibrant cultural scene. Tours make for a more personalized encounter by sharing personal tales in addition to information. It is a handy place for going off the usual tourist route since it's just a short stroll from the French Quarter. The museum is open from 10am to 4pm (closed on Sundays and Mondays), and is a perfect place for learning more about the lesser-known but very significant facets of New Orleans' history.

Outdoor Activities and Adventures

Guests can enjoy a wide variety of outdoor activities in New Orleans for taking in the city's history, vibrant culture, and natural beauty with lots of choices to get in touch with nature, strolling around the city and taking in beautiful parks.

- **New Orleans City Park**

A vast 1,300-acre urban paradise, New Orleans City Park is teeming with adventure, culture, and wildlife. With its picturesque pathways, serene ponds, and stately oak trees providing a serene background, this famous green park is ideal for excitement and leisure. Wander through the wacky Storyland amusement park, visit the charming New Orleans Botanical Garden, or take in the magnificent sculpture garden and artwork at the New Orleans Museum of Art. The park's many areas make it the perfect place for solitary nature retreats, informal adventures, and family picnics. City Park offers a range of leisure opportunities to accommodate all interests in addition to its natural beauty. Disc golfers, fishermen, and paddle boaters can enjoy the peaceful lakes, while families can have a little fun at the on-site amusement park or on the miniature train. It's ideal for pet owners as well because of the expansive areas and dog run. The park is easily accessible by the city's trolley system and is open every day from 5 AM to 10 PM. A stress-free stay is guaranteed by the restrooms and plenty of parking.

- **Crescent Park**

Along the banks of the Mississippi River, Crescent Park at *Crescent Park Trail, 2300 N Peters St, New Orleans, LA 70117,* provides a tranquil haven with some of the most breathtaking views of the city's cityscape. Visitors will enjoy a peaceful respite from the bustle of the city by walking, jogging, or cycling along this 1.4-mile asphalt track. Following the river's curvature, the park's winding walk creates a picturesque trail dotted with wildflowers, native plants, and comfortable picnic areas. Convenient drinking fountains and portable bathrooms are positioned around the route to guarantee a pleasant stay. The park is easily accessible across the railway thanks to a pedestrian bridge with an elevator that makes it available to everyone. Crescent Park offers both open areas and peaceful spots for rest, fusing contemporary architecture with the beauty of nature. Pets are welcome in the small dog run, and there is room for sports, skating, and community gatherings in the spacious, shaded warehouse area. The park is the ideal location for morning jogs or evening walks since it is open every day from 6 AM to 7:30 PM. Guests should keep in mind to carry drinks and sunscreen for daytime trips since summer days may become quite hot.

- **Jean Lafitte National Historical Park and Preserve**

For a day excursion from New Orleans, Jean Lafitte National Historical Park and Preserve is a fascinating place with a rich tapestry of nature and history. The park is about 25 minutes southwest of the city, and comprises more than 23,000 acres of

woods, marshes, and wetlands. Visitors can experience a range of activities at its many tourist centers, which include the Barataria Preserve. The park is well-known for its picturesque boat cruises that meander through the expansive marsh area, offering a chance to see the area's distinctive species, including alligators, herons, and other birds, in their native environment. Trails for bicyclists and hikers meander through verdant surroundings, enabling guests to experience the tranquility of nature while discovering the region's rich cultural legacy.

The Chalmette Battlefield, the location of the renowned Battle of New Orleans in 1815, is one of the important historical sites of Jean Lafitte National Historical Park, also known for its natural beauty. The Chalmette National Cemetery that commemorates those who participated in this crucial fight, gives a counterpart to the battlefield.

The park's cultural centers provide information on the traditions and practices that defined the area while showcasing the legacy of the local people. It's simple to get to the park; just take LA-46 or US-90 from New Orleans, and you'll be rewarded with a beautiful trip that takes you to this amazing historical and ecological treasure.

- **New Orleans Botanical Garden**

The New Orleans Botanical Garden, located at *5 Victory Ave, New Orleans, LA 70119,* within City Park, offers a tranquil escape filled with natural beauty and artistic touches. Open daily from 10 AM to 4:30 PM, with entry tickets starting at $12 per person, the garden is a haven for plant lovers and casual visitors alike. It features an impressive collection of exotic species, including vibrant orchids, fragrant verbena, and striking cacti, as well as themed gardens like serene Japanese landscapes. Seasonal plant sales also give visitors the chance to take home a piece of this lush paradise. The garden's sculptures, including works by Enrique Alferez, add a layer of artistic charm to the experience, making every path and archway feel like a scene from a movie; ideal for photography enthusiasts. Beyond its botanical wonders, the garden offers a relaxing setting with shaded areas, swings, and peaceful spots to sit and enjoy a coffee or iced tea. Families with children can explore Storyland, a whimsical playground located next to the garden (additional entry fee applies), with fun activities for younger visitors.

Family-Friendly Activities

Families can enjoy a range of exciting activities in New Orleans that are sure to delight both children and adults. The city combines entertainment, education, and culture via interactive museums and outdoor experiences. With its exciting rides and serene parks, New Orleans is a great place for families of all ages to visit.

- **Louisiana Children's Museum**

The 8.5 acres of indoor and outdoor displays of the Louisiana Children's Museum situated at *15 Henry Thomas Dr, New Orleans, LA 70124,* are intended to stimulate creativity, inquiry, and education. The Helis Foundation's Art For All program offers free entrance to Louisiana citizens on the second Sunday of every other month, while entry prices start at $18 per person. With features like water play, painting classes, and pretend role-playing

areas, the museum's displays are well-thought-out and suitable for kids of all ages. Kids can engage with nature in the lush outdoor areas, and they can see exhibitions like Dig Into Nature, Make Your Mark, and Move with the River in the inside areas. Families will enjoy the captivating combination of educational activities that skillfully combine creativity and enjoyment for hours on end.

While kids explore anything from a building block area and a veterinarian clinic to a fun kitchen and grocery shop layout, parents can unwind. While larger children may get their hands dirty in the painting studios, music rooms, and water features, younger guests will adore the designated toddler areas. Parents will also find ample seats in the museum, with huge windows overlooking peaceful scenery like a nearby pond and weeping willows. Lunch at the museum is convenient since the café offers kid-friendly fare.

- **Storyland**

Tucked at *5 Victory Ave, New Orleans, LA 70124*, Storyland offers a mystical experience full of vibrant sculptures, engaging playscapes, and well-known fictional characters. This creative outdoor attraction is perfect for families with little children or anybody wishing to lose themselves in a realm of nostalgia, and admission costs start at $6 per person. Storyland is open every day except Mondays from 10 AM to 4:30 PM, and allows visitors to enter life-sized settings from beloved stories. This magical place encourages imagination and adventure in every corner.

Storyland, intended to entertain both kids and adults, combines narrative with play to create an experience that will never be forgotten. While adults explore the grounds with drinks in hand; the park permits beer and wine on-site, children can enjoy interactive activities and climbing structures. With so many spaces to explore, Storyland fosters creativity everywhere, making it the ideal setting for making enjoyable memories. It's a welcoming haven for families where kids can let off steam in a pleasant and safe setting while parents can take part in the activities or relax in the shade.

- **Audubon Aquarium**

- For guests of all ages, the Audubon Aquarium of the Americas situated at *1 Canal St, New Orleans, LA 70130,* presents an enthralling voyage under the seas, teeming with marine life and interactive displays. The aquarium welcomes visitors to explore its 400,000-gallon Gulf of Mexico display, home to enormous sharks, tarpon, rays, and other aquatic species, with admission prices beginning at $35 per person.

The walk-through tunnel that brings the bright Caribbean reef to life and provides a captivating view of stingrays flying above and colorful fish darting through the water, is one of the highlights. Plus, visitors can interact directly with marine life by seeing playful sea otters and handling stingrays. Through exhibits on the Audubon's work to rescue and rehabilitate marine animals and sea turtles for release into the wild, visitors are exposed to the organization's dedication to conservation beyond the maritime exhibits. The aquarium creates a fully comprehensive experience by providing access to a tranquil butterfly garden and an insectarium full of intriguing creatures in addition to aquatic adventures. The displays include terrestrial species like owls and eagles in addition to marine life that heightens the sense of amazement. The aquarium is a great way to spend a day because of its family-friendly features, professional personnel, and well-maintained animal habitats. With convenient parking close by, it's the perfect place to escape the heat or rain and it's open everyday from 10 AM to 5 PM.

- **Carousel Gardens Amusement Park**

With admission prices beginning at $25 per person, Carousel Gardens Amusement Park situated at *7 Victory Ave, New Orleans, LA 70124*, provides a beautiful blend of historic elegance and excitement. The park offers pleasure for kids and adults with 16 rides, including an old-fashioned wooden carousel with exquisitely designed horses. The park's focal point, this famous carousel has been enthralling guests for many years with its elaborate design and  classic charm. Families can enjoy the fun together since many rides allow smaller children to ride with an adult companion. Although it costs extra, the park also provides a vintage train trip around the grounds, giving the visit a more relaxed feel. As the seasons change, Carousel Gardens' ambiance becomes even more enchanting at special occasions like Christmas, when it is transformed as part of the Celebration in the Oaks event. Beyond the rides, the park is open all day due to its close proximity to Storyland and the botanical garden.

The adjacent botanical garden offers a tranquil haven, while Storyland, with its fanciful fairy-tale constructions, contributes to the lively atmosphere. Weekends are the best times to visit the park since it is open from 11 AM to 6 PM every day and is closed on Mondays and Tuesdays. With its assortment of rides, open-air attractions, and welcoming personnel, Carousel Gardens provides a nostalgic experience that transports visitors to a happier, more carefree era.

A CULINARY JOURNEY THROUGH NEW ORLEANS

Sweet Delights & Recipes to Sample

With its unique combination of French, African, Spanish, and Creole flavors, New Orleans is a gastronomic haven where each meal tells a tale. Food is more than simply sustenance while visiting the city; it's an experience. It would be like missing half the city's experience if you skipped its sweets, as legendary as its music.

A trip to New Orleans wouldn't be complete without indulging in a beignet. Best eaten hot and fresh, these square pieces of fried dough are heavily coated with powdered sugar. Though numerous cafés across the city offer their variants, two excellent places to taste them are Café du Monde and Morning Call. Praline, a classic Southern confection composed with pecans, sugar, butter, and cream, is another treat. It is the ideal snack to purchase from candy stores located around the French Quarter because of its nutty sweetness and melt-in-your-mouth quality. A sno-ball can satisfy your need for something refreshing, particularly in the hot months. These cool snacks made from finely shaved ice and topped with flavoring syrups (and sometimes condensed milk) are sold at stalls all around the city. Locals love Hansen's Sno-Bliz and Plum Street Snowballs.

New Orleans' savory cuisine is just as well-known as its sweets. A must-try, gumbo is a spicy stew prepared with sausage, okra, or shrimp that differs somewhat depending on where you get it and every variation provides a different twist. Another popular dish is jambalaya, which combines rice, spices, sausage, and seafood to create a flavorful and substantial meal. Try a po' boy, a traditional sandwich made with French bread, fried shrimp, roast beef, or other contents and topped with mayo, lettuce, and tomato, if you're feeling really daring. Red beans and rice, which are often eaten on Mondays, are a hearty staple that offers a deeper exploration of regional cuisines. They are sometimes cooked with ham or sausage for hours to acquire its rich flavor.

New Orleans' seafood merits its own special attention. Seafood enthusiasts should try the chargrilled oysters, grilled to perfection and served with Parmesan and garlic butter. They were made famous by Drago's Seafood Restaurant, but several other restaurants have mastered this buttery, smokey treat. A bowl of crawfish étouffée that layers crawfish tails in a roux-based sauce and serves it over rice, offers strong Creole tastes if you're craving something lighter. Locals get together for crawfish boils, when the crustaceans are cooked with potatoes, corn, and a variety of seasonings, when crawfish season arrives.

A traditional bread pudding, a dessert fashioned from leftover bread soaked in custard, baked, and topped with a rich rum sauce, is a great way to round off your culinary adventure. If you're going during Mardi Gras season, you also can choose a piece of king cake. With frosting and multicolored sugar on top, this festive pastry packed with cinnamon conceals a little plastic baby that represents positive fortune.

Top Eats and Restaurants

New Orleans is a food lover's dream, with flavors as vibrant and diverse as its culture. Be it fresh seafood, hearty Creole dishes, or soul-soothing comfort food, the city offers something to please every appetite. The dining scene ranges from refined eateries to bustling neighborhood spots where meals are served with warmth and flair:

- **Parkway Bakery & Tavern**

Serving some of the greatest po' boys in New Orleans, Parkway Bakery & Tavern located at *538 Hagan Ave, New Orleans, LA 70119*, has been a treasured neighborhood mainstay since 1911. This relaxed location provides the ideal fusion of history and taste, complete with a gorgeous terrace, lots of free parking, and a comfortable inside environment. Open every day except Mondays and Tuesdays from 10 a.m. to 6 p.m., it is still a must-visit for tasting real New Orleans food. Parkway, well-known for its traditional po' boys, serves a variety of contents on soft, crispy French bread, including freshly fried Gulf shrimp and delicious roast beef covered in flavorful gravy. With fresh lettuce, tomato, and Creole mustard on top, the Impossible Burger po' boy is a tasty choice for plant-based eaters. With most things costing between $10 and $20, the menu offers substantial servings that are reasonably priced and satisfying.

Comforting sides like jambalaya and mixed fries are popular options, as is the surf-and-turf po' boy, a rich blend of fried shrimp and roast beef. Additionally, Parkway is well-known for its bread pudding, a delightful way to cap off a substantial dinner. Although there isn't a special children's menu, families can still enjoy dishes like beef hot dogs and toasted cheese sandwiches. Beyond the cuisine, Parkway is a welcoming place for both residents and visitors due to its laid-back atmosphere, welcoming staff, and immaculate amenities. The experience is completed with an ice-cold beer or a frozen porch swing drink, perfectly encapsulating casual dining in New Orleans.

- **Liuzza's by the Track**

A short stroll from City Park, Liuzza's by the Track is a welcoming, laid-back Creole pub located at *1518 N Lopez St, New Orleans, LA 70119*, next to the New Orleans Fairgrounds. Although the building itself is from the 1930s, which adds to its elegance, this neighborhood treasure has been serving hearty, savory cuisine since 1996. It is a popular destination for both residents and tourists, particularly during the Jazz and Heritage Festival, and is well-known for its relaxed ambiance with soft lighting, walls covered with old photographs, and welcoming staff.

It's a terrific place to get robust New Orleans favorites at affordable costs, with meals costing from $10 to $20 per item. It's open every day from 11 a.m. to 8 p.m. (except on Sundays). Their famous BBQ shrimp po' boy, a rich, saucy dish full of delicate shrimp, is one of the menu's hallmark po' boys. Crispy fried green tomatoes, slow-cooked corned beef, and seafood-rich gumbo with a well-balanced roux are some well-liked choices. The fried oyster po' boys and crawfish étouffée are other popular choices for trying additional Creole tastes. A cool beer in a big chalice goes well with any dinner, and the enormous onion rings make a filling appetizer. The genuine, down-to-earth comfort cuisine served at Liuzza's by the Track captures the spirit of New Orleans dining.

- **Domilise's Po-Boys & Bar**

Since 1924, Domilise's Po-Boys & Bar has been a treasured local institution that has delighted customers with its enormous po' boys and laid-back vibe. This restaurant, housed at *5240 Annunciation St, New Orleans, LA 70115,* in a straightforward counter-serve area, embodies traditional New Orleans eating, where cuisine is made fresh and to order. It encourages visitors to take their time and savor the experience and is open every day from 11 a.m. to 3 p.m (closed on Sundays). The fried oyster po' boy is a popular choice among the menu's assortment of po' boys that range in price from $10

66

to $20. The roast beef po' boy, served generously with thick sauce that makes every mouthful unforgettable, and is a local favorite. The restaurant's quaint, retro décor enhances its allure by bringing guests back in time with a nostalgic atmosphere. The little corner patio provides a pleasant place to have a relaxing drink while you wait for your dinner, despite the limited seating. Good cuisine takes time, so it's not uncommon for service to be a little sluggish, but it adds to the charm.

- **Café du Monde**

Located at *800 Decatur Street*, Café du Monde is a famous New Orleans landmark that has been entertaining visitors with its chicory coffee, beignets, and café au laits since 1862. This busy café is open every day from 9am. to 5pm, and is well-known for its lively street life and relaxed vibe. The menu is small, with coffee drinks ranging from $2 to $5 and beignets costing around $3 for three. This makes it a reasonably priced treat.

Beyond its delicious food, Café du Monde's attractiveness lies in its vibrant atmosphere that is often enhanced by local musicians performing outdoors. The line goes steadily, enabling customers to savor the anticipation of their delicacies. Remember that Café du Monde only accepts cash; therefore, it is best to carry some cash with you when you visit. Savoring the warm beignets, which are best had right away after being presented, is an enjoyable experience that perfectly embodies New Orleans culture.

- **Coop's Place**

Situated at *1109 Decatur St, New Orleans, LA 70116*, Coop's Place is a laid-back Cajun and Creole eatery that is well-liked for its simple eating experience. This lively restaurant, which is solely for adults and is open every day at 11 a.m., is well-known for its humorous but welcoming staff and extensive menu of delectable homemade food. Menu dishes usually cost between $20 and $30, and is a wonderful deal considering the quality of the meal. Showcasing the rich tastes of Cajun food, the specialty sausage and rabbit jambalaya, smoked duck quesadilla, and fried chicken are some of the highlights. The relaxed setting is ideal for dining or getting a drink from the well-stocked bar that serves cool beers and drinks to go with the substantial fare. Even with its modest decor, Coop's Place offers a memorable eating experience. It's a terrific place for a fast snack and a relaxing evening because of the lively environment. The restaurant's dedication to providing delectable, comfortable cuisine is shown by favorites like the coops sample plate and the BBQ shrimp on French bread.

- **The Joint**

Barbecue enthusiasts should not miss The Joint, well-known for its slow-smoked meats and substantial side dishes. This eccentric, cypress-paneled restaurant is open every day from 11:30 a.m. to 9 p.m. (closed on Sundays), and has a relaxed vibe that goes well with its food. Items typically cost between $10 and $20, which is excellent value given their quality and serving sizes. Along with delectable ribs, sausage, and a choice of sides like red potato salad and cornbread that complete the meal, diners will gush over the pulled

pork that has the ideal taste balance without being too fatty or salty. The welcoming full bar enhances the whole experience by serving up cool beverages like sangria daiquiris. The menu offers a variety of smoked meats, such as burnt ends and brisket, that are all masterfully cooked to bring out their rich characteristics. The sides, including baked beans, macaroni and cheese, and a zesty coleslaw that goes well with the smokey meats, are as outstanding. The welcoming personnel adds to the welcoming atmosphere, making each visit delightful. For some of the greatest BBQ in the city, the odd fly may buzz about, but that's a minor inconvenience.

- **Dat Dog**

With meals priced between $10 and $20, Dat Dog is a lively neighborhood staple that is well-known for its inventive hot dogs, sausages, and vegetarian selections. With unusual ingredients including alligator, duck, and crawfish sausages, this vibrant counter-serve restaurant, opens every day at 11 a.m., gives a fun take on traditional cuisine. "Jimmy's Chicago Dog," loaded with well-known Midwest ingredients, and "Rougarou," prepared with alligator sausage, are popular options. Every mouthful of Dat Dog is made even more decadent by the buns that are more akin to warm, pillowy bread. Their cheesy tater tots and loaded fries go well with the main courses, and the complete bar serves beverages to go with the meal.

Dat Dog offers a pleasant place to savor strong tastes and a delightful diversion from the heat thanks to its vibrant décor and laid-back vibe. Friendly service and a cheerful atmosphere greet visitors. Because it combines local flare with street-side charm, the Frenchmen Street location is particularly well-liked.

- **Juan's Flying Burrito - CBD**

The Central Business District's (CBD) Juan's Flying Burrito serves a daring blend of Mexican cuisine with a distinctly New Orleans flair. This lively and  colorful restaurant serves a range of freshly prepared, flavorful dishes that range in price from $10 to $20. Blackened fish tacos and the famous "Flying Burrito," stuffed with shrimp, chicken, and beef, are two dishes that have strong Creole influences. To ensure that there is something for everyone, the menu also offers taco salads, quesadillas, and hefty meat fajitas. Each mouthful is wonderfully complemented by the distinctive kick that the house-made green salsa imparts.

Juan's Flying Burrito is well-known for its hearty servings and vibrant, laid-back ambiance that elevate eating beyond a simple meal. A satisfying appetizer that sets the tone for the remainder of the dinner is the trio of chips with guacamole, salsa, and queso. Cocktails created to reflect the lively spirit of the restaurant are served freely, along with tequilas, mezcals, and margaritas. It is a handy place to stop for lunch or a late dinner, and it is open every day from 11 a.m. to 10 p.m.

JAZZ & LIVE MUSIC EXPERIENCES

There is music wherever you look in New Orleans, a city that is teeming with the spirit of jazz. It's a center for fans of both jazz and blues, and you can take in live performances that highlight the city's extensive musical past. There's always something unique to experience here, and these are a few of the top places for experiencing those remarkable experiences:

- **The Spotted Cat Music Club**

Nestled at *623 Frenchmen St, New Orleans, LA 70117*, The Spotted Cat Music Club captures the essence of New Orleans's rich jazz legacy in a vibrant, intimate setting. This well-liked venue has a naturally genuine appeal that attracts a varied audience of residents and guests with its worn-out bar and little, snug stage. Open every day from 2 pm to 2 am; it's the ideal place to genuinely feel the pulse of the city. Here, when performers mount the stage to blast the crowd with vivid sounds, the low lighting and mixed décor provide a nostalgic background. The atmosphere inside, despite its small footprint, is friendly and energizing, beckoning everyone to assemble around for a close-knit, standing-room-only experience akin to a private performance.

Every evening at The Spotted Cat presents a fresh jazz experience. With classic New Orleans jazz, blues, swing and funk, the roster has gifted players with individual styles that provide an amazing range of sound to the stage. Priced from $10 to $20, drinks keep spirits high, and the energetic audience frequently overflows onto the dance floor, swaying to the music and contributing to the dynamic mood. The laid-back, understated environment of the Spotted Cat lets one personally engage with the music, therefore generating an immersive experience that really captures the spirit of New Orleans.

- **Snug Harbor Jazz Bistro**

Snug Harbor Jazz Bistro is a New Orleans gem,  flawlessly merging live jazz with upgraded Creole food in an evocative 1800s-era architecture. Located at *626 Frenchmen St, New Orleans, LA 70116*, this legendary institution has become a go-to location for jazz fans and cuisine lovers alike. With three unique areas; a dining room, a bar, and an intimate music room. Open every day from 5 p.m. to midnight, it's a great stop for experiencing a deep dive into New Orleans culture. The dining area offers up premium Creole cuisine in the $30 to $50 range, masterfully mixing the traditional tastes of the region with an upgraded presentation, while the sounds of live jazz flow through, giving warmth and energy to the setting.

What sets Snug Harbor apart is its tiny music room, a brick-walled refuge where jazz takes center stage. With top-notch acoustics, the space delivers a premium listening experience for soothing jazz classics as well as daring, contemporary renditions by local luminaries and worldwide artists alike. The attentive staff creates a flawless experience, enabling guests to concentrate exclusively on the wonder of the music and the great cuisine. For visitors wishing to genuinely experience the pulse of New Orleans, Snug Harbor delivers an authentic and unique journey, combining the finest Creole food, outstanding service, and a world-class jazz ambiance.

- **Tipitina's**

Tipitina's is an iconic New Orleans institution, where the passion of live music and Cajun dance comes to life in a rustic, black-and-white tiled warehouse area. Established in 1977 by a group of dedicated music fans, Tipitina was designed to celebrate the renowned Professor Longhair and his immortal composition "Tipitina," throughout the years, it has become a lighthouse for both up-and-coming musicians and established stars. The theater serves as a monument of New Orleans' musical heritage, presenting notable artists from the city and beyond. Tipitina has always maintained loyalty to its origins, giving a genuine and energetic experience with musicians spanning genres and cultures. The unusual mood here seems like walking into a musical celebration that has been blooming for decades, making it a must-visit for experiencing the city's music industry at its heart. The experience at Tipitina's is as raw and compelling as the history behind its walls. The facility is famed for its Free Friday concerts in the summer when residents and tourists congregate to dance and enjoy live acts. A night at Tipitina's is packed with energy, friendship, and spirit, heightened by a setting intended for both music and memories. Since being bought by the New Orleans-based band Galactic in 2018, Tipitina has maintained loyalty to its goal, fostering local talent while pulling in national and international artists to its stage.

- **The Maison**

The Maison on Frenchmen Street is a bustling, three-level music venue and restaurant that reflects the exuberant atmosphere of New Orleans with its constant program of jazz, funk, and blues on numerous stages. Open seven days a week, The Maison attracts residents and visitors alike, guaranteeing a genuine musical encounter every night of the week. Known for its laid-back feel and welcoming setting, the venue welcomes guests to enjoy live music from a variety of stages, drink traditional New Orleans cocktails like Old Fashioneds and Sazeracs, and relax amid the Frenchmen Street scene. Without any cover fee, it's simple to drop by and explore the night.

With a range of seating choices, the Maison provides a setting that's as versatile as its guests. The tiny upstairs section offers a calmer setting if requested, making it excellent for individuals who prefer a bit more relaxed experience without missing the music. Known for its open and warm setting, the venue especially caters to families, enabling everyone to enjoy the enchantment of New Orleans jazz together. The food selection may be limited, but The Maison is a go-to for music and beverages, giving an immersive opportunity to connect with the city's pulse.

- **Blue Nile**

The Blue Nile on Frenchmen Street is a cornerstone of New Orleans' live music culture, presenting an amazing combination of jazz, funk, blues, and brass that embodies the city's spirit. Open every day (except Tuesdays), this iconic club brings music enthusiasts into an intimate setting packed with vivid sounds and an inviting spirit. The club has two levels, each with its atmosphere; the main floor is where musicians bring the audience alive, with a mix of people and ages enjoying a soulful evening together.

Upstairs, themed evenings add a layer of excitement, showcasing events like reggae and brass, making every visit to Blue Nile a new musical excursion. It's a great area to relax with beautifully made beverages, all while immersing yourself in a historic New Orleans environment. The ambiance at Blue Nile is as much about community as it is about music. The crew contributes warmth and charm to the experience, making visitors feel right at home in the center of this busy music scene. The bar provides a choice of drinks, expertly prepared to complement the beat of the live acts that keep the excitement high late into the night. Even early in the evening, the arena crackles with an electric vibe, with bands offering energetic performances that span classic jazz standards as well as bouncy funk tracks.

- **d.b.a.**

D.B.A., tucked at *618 Frenchmen St, New Orleans, LA 70116,* presents an intimate and dynamic venue for enjoying live music with a genuine New Orleans edge. Open every day from 4 PM to 3 AM, this intimate, smoke-free pub blends a terrific sound system with a varied roster of local and regional artists. Known for featuring jazz, blues, and soul bands, D.B.A. brings the city's music culture to life each night with passionate performances and an audience eager to enjoy the ambiance. Despite the modest size, there's ample space to come near the stage, offering an up-close, immersive experience that makes every concert special. With no cover fee, it's simple to wander in and let the music sweep you up in the environment, all while enjoying a finely designed drink selection that sticks out. Behind the bar, a top-notch variety of craft beers, wine, and spirits caters to a spectrum of preferences, bringing a touch of refinement to this down-to-earth restaurant. For a sophisticated taste, D.B.A. even offers rare, high-quality bourbons, allowing guests the opportunity to sample something genuinely remarkable in a vibrant atmosphere. The bartenders keep the cocktails flowing with expertise and friendliness, accentuating the inviting mood that makes D.B.A. an institution on Frenchmen Street. It's a fantastic setting to drink perfectly crafted cocktails or draft beers while the music weaves through the crowd, converting a casual evening into a uniquely New Orleans experience.

- **House of Blues Restaurant & Bar**

The House of Blues Restaurant & Bar at *225 Decatur St, New Orleans, LA 70130,* is a top venue for experiencing an immersive evening of Southern

comfort cuisine, refreshing cocktails, and spectacular live music. This rock and blues-themed institution marries its typical Southern charm with a menu filled with mouth-watering foods, from po' boys to spicy jambalaya. Nestled in the middle of the city, House of Blues allows visitors to relax and enjoy a delectable dinner while the sounds of live blues, rock, and jazz fill the air. Every aspect, the rustic design and the wall art, offers a one-of-a-kind experience that pays respect to music and Southern culture.

Just beyond is the Voodoo Garden, a mysterious outdoor spot where visitors may drink cocktails and absorb the distinct feel of New Orleans. With seating for nearly 1,800 people, the House of Blues can accommodate everyone but retains an intimate feel with top-notch acoustics and a pleasant ambiance. Even before the music begins, perusing the quirky design and antique posters on the walls makes for a fascinating experience.

- **Three Muses**

Three Muses located at *536 Frenchmen St, New Orleans, LA 70116,* is a jewel that marries live jazz, worldwide small dishes, and house-crafted drinks in an intimate, air-conditioned atmosphere, making it great for a pleasant night out in New Orleans. This tiny bar and bistro delivers a vibe that feels both refined and warm, with a carefully picked roster of local jazz ensembles presenting live music weekly.

Each band offers a distinct rhythm to the environment, making it a must-visit for music enthusiasts who wish to experience the true jazz scene of Frenchmen Street. The room itself is small, bringing a personal touch to each performance, and the attentive, pleasant personnel ensure that visitors feel right at home. On the culinary side, Three Muses offers a menu of internationally-inspired small meals, great for tasting and sharing. Crowd favorites include delicious pig debris po'boys, crunchy cauliflower nibbles, and a luscious chicken sandwich, each brimming with flavor and tailored to combine wonderfully with the distinctive drinks on offer. The Muse cocktail, particularly for gin fans, is a popular option, displaying the bar's attention to quality and inventiveness.

- **Maple Leaf Bar**

Maple Leaf Bar is a treasured institution at *8316 Oak St, New Orleans, LA 70118*, recognized for its colorful atmosphere and rich musical heritage. With its unique tin roof and busy dance floor, this institution has been a favorite with residents and tourists alike for decades. Open every day, it presents an eclectic mix of live New Orleans-style music, making it a go-to for experiencing a genuine nightlife away from the touristic bustle of Bourbon Street. The bar's vast outside space, filled with trees and seats, offers a comfortable respite for enjoying a drink in the fresh air while still being part of the excitement inside. Guests can anticipate an intimate encounter at Maple Leaf, frequently finding themselves only a few steps away from the artists, creating an

85

electrifying connection that increases the pleasure of the events. The bartenders are recognized for their warmth and efficiency, ensuring that everyone can keep their drinks flowing while they immerse themselves in the music.

- **Bacchanal Fine Wine & Spirits**

Bacchanal Fine Wine & Spirits is a pleasant hideaway nestled at *600 Poland Ave, New Orleans, LA 70117*, providing an experience that flawlessly mixes wine, cuisine, and live music. This unusual location functions as both a wine-and-cheese shop and a bustling meeting area, where customers can indulge in internationally-themed small meals while taking in the lively environment. Visitors can make their charcuterie boards, picking from an incredible choice of meats and cheeses, nicely matched by a range of fresh bread and dried fruits. The joy of Bacchanal resides not only in the appetizing food but also in the sensation of filling a bucket with ice to keep their selected wines cool. The facility offers an enticing terrace decorated with lush foliage, where clients can relax and enjoy live music performances, making it a wonderful setting for a casual excursion with friends or a romantic evening under the stars. The environment at Bacchanal is simply wonderful, reinforced by the pleasant and experienced staff who are always ready to propose the finest wine pairings. The venue's arrangement is especially unique, with a wine store below and pleasant dining spaces above, allowing for both networking and private chats. Regular live music events add to the appeal, making it a popular destination.

HIDDEN GEMS AND OFF-THE-BEATEN-PATH ACTIVITIES

New Orleans is teeming with hidden jewels and unusual locales that go beyond the traditional attractions, presenting a look into the city's original charm and dynamic energy. These off-the-beaten-path sites enable visitors to experience New Orleans like a native, and exploring these hidden jewels shows a side of the city that's packed with character, creativity, and history, great for digging further into its culture:

- **Music Box Village**

Music Box Village is a lively and innovative retreat into a world of interactive art and music. Tucked at *4557 N Rampart St, New Orleans, LA 70117,* away from the normal tourist trails, this unusual "village" is made up of musical dwellings, each constructed by craftsmen to function as both an instrument and an architectural marvel. Inspired by New Orleans' rich musical and cultural past, the residences encourage guests to explore and create songs by

touching, tapping, and playing practically every surface. Each building vibrates with its musical voice, through fanciful railings that ring with sound to steps that hum underfoot. Open Fridays through Sundays, this artist-built paradise is a favorite for families, musicians, and art enthusiasts alike, giving an extraordinary playground for both adults and children. Visitors will witness the ingenuity that feeds the local art scene while immersing themselves in a combination of architecture and music unlike any other.

More than a static art installation, Music Box Village provides live concerts, artist residencies, and creative workshops, frequently utilizing interactive structures as part of the event. The venue, a flagship initiative of the artist-led New Orleans Airlift, typically contains an outdoor artist market and offers a range of creative drinks from a full bar, making it a great area to chill while exploring and playing with music. Frequent activities, drum circles and performance art, enable visitors to meet with local and international artists in an intimate environment.

- **Longue Vue House and Gardens**

Longue Vue House & Gardens is an amazing 8-acre estate that offers a trip through beauty, history, and art. Nestled at *7 Bamboo Rd, New Orleans, LA 70124*, this 1940s house and garden sanctuary opens daily to visitors eager to explore its magnificent interiors and perfectly planned gardens. With admission prices beginning at $21 per person, all are welcomed into an exquisite world where historical design, magnificent art, and breathtaking architecture blend in every area.

The estate's guided tours show the interesting heritage of the family who once called it home, their contributions to the community, and the unique architectural decisions that brought the house to life. Comprising vast rooms with exquisite architectural elements and corridors packed with artwork, the house highlights the riches and mysteries of a former age, delivering an intriguing experience for history lovers and architecture aficionados alike. Beyond the home, Longue Vue's grounds are a masterpiece of landscape design, with bright flower beds, fountains, ponds, and themed gardens that capture nature's grandeur and provide great picture opportunities. Strolling along the oak-lined walks, visitors find a variety of plant life, well-maintained flower gardens, and tranquil spots that promote rest and appreciation. For families with kids, there's a well-planned playground, making Longue Vue fun for all ages. Friendly and informed personnel contribute to the welcome ambiance, frequently giving insights about the estate's history and horticulture. A trip to the beautiful gift store closes up the tour, giving unique souvenirs and presents to remember this wonderful spot.

- **The Carousel Bar & Lounge**

The Carousel Bar & Lounge at the Hotel Monteleone is a treasured New Orleans jewel, marrying historical elegance with an enticing twist. Open every day from 11 am to midnight, this landmark venue sets up a unique experience with its circular bar that gently turns like a carousel, encouraging  customers to delve into a world of whimsy and Southern elegance. The bar's design reflects an older age, with a hint of antique flair and a sophisticated atmosphere, offering an excellent background for sipping a martini. Positioned near the band area, luxurious sofas provide warm seating with front-row views of live music, adding an energizing, immersive element to your stay. With pricing ranging between $20 and $30 per person, the experience seems both affordable and special.

Drinks at The Carousel Bar & Lounge are made with attention to detail and innovation, each beverage reflecting the abilities of its professional bartenders. The menu includes local favorites like the Sazerac, as well as creative, seasonal cocktails that make the most of fresh, regional ingredients. Through perfectly blended Plantation Old Fashioneds to refreshing glasses of Pinot Grigio, the diversity guarantees that there's something to suit every taste. The bustling and casual ambiance, complemented by live jazz or soulful performances, gives an extra layer of pleasure to each visit, making it simple to immerse yourself in conversation and music.

- **Faulkner House Books**

Nestled in a lovely 1837 townhouse along Pirate Alley, Faulkner House Books located at *624 Pirates Alley, New Orleans, LA 70116*, welcomes guests to walk into a realm of literary history and uncommon discovery. Once the abode of William Faulkner himself, who made his first novel inside these walls, the building today serves as a treasure trove of books specialized in southern literature, classics, poetry, and modern fiction.

With a selective collection of new, rare, and autographed editions, this small bookshop distinguishes out as a distinctive destination in New Orleans. The modest area, packed to the brim with well-selected books, creates an ambiance that balances the elegance of the past with the appeal of literary discovery. For those who respect reading, passing through this old gateway seems like stepping into a bygone period, where each shelf is arranged with a feeling of regard for the written word. Open every day from 10 a.m. to 5 p.m., Faulkner House Books permits up to six people inside at a time, guaranteeing a calm browsing experience. The front rooms of the store, although small in size, are crammed with a great selection of books, local interest nonfiction as well as wonderfully bound versions of classic stories.

Knowledgeable staff members are on hand, ready to make thoughtful suggestions or provide insights into the most distinctive products available. Beyond its literary offers, the bookstore's aura is heightened by its vintage design and proximity to the bustling of the French Quarter. A visit here is a voyage through Southern literary tradition, a celebration of Faulkner's legacy, and a calm, atmospheric vacation suitable for book fans seeking something unique.

- **The Singing Oak**

Located at *New Orleans, LA 70124,* inside City Park, the Singing Oak is a calm haven where art and nature mix in a musical display. Large, finely tuned wind chimes on this big oak tree create mesmerizing tunes whenever a breeze blows through. Nestled next to Big Lake on Zemurray Trail, this little wonder draws guests wanting peace away from the busy city. Every chime is exactly tuned to make a harmonic scale, thereby turning the stirring wind into an organic melody. Visitors sitting under this tree will enjoy the serene, almost otherworldly tones of the chimes that change yet beautifully with the breeze.

With easy access 24 hours a day, the Singing Oak is worth seeing especially on a windy day when the chimes are most busy. Keep in mind there are no seats straight beneath, so bringing a blanket to lay out on the grass will make for a perfect day or evening. Visitors will find it right off the path going toward the New Orleans Museum of Art, surrounded by City Park's tall live oaks. The tree is a great place for shots as its shade against the sky gives the experience a beautiful aspect at sunset.

- **Parleaux Beer Lab**

Parleaux Beer Lab, hidden at *634 Lesseps St, New Orleans, LA 70117,* in the lively Bywater area, is a must-visit for exploring the imaginative side of the city's craft beer sector. This welcome "beer lab" provides a lively, family-friendly setting where guests can relax and taste a changing range of clever small-batch beers. True to New Orleans' varied culture, Parleaux's beer range includes a broad array of types, powerful IPAs, smooth stouts, refreshing sours and experimental beers that push the limits of traditional beer traditions.

With 12 taps that change often, each visit offers something new and interesting to enjoy, along with the chance to take home specialty bottles, four-packs, or even unique branded goods. Their outdoor beer garden provides a wide, dog-friendly area perfect for meeting with friends or having a laid-back day with family. The experience at Parleaux Beer Lab is also about community and local culture. The cheerful personnel and their great knowledge of each brew make picking a flight a pleasant aspect of the visit, and food trucks regularly park outside, giving excellent local nibbles to match the beer. The environment is lively and down-to-earth, with kids and dogs enjoying the outside deck as people drink and talk.

- **St. Roch Market**

St. Roch Market is a famous food market with a rich past dating back to 1875, reborn today as a lively culinary draw. Located at *2381 St Claude Ave, New Orleans, LA 70117,* in an ancient market building, with a broad array of food sellers that reflect both local and foreign cuisines. Visitors can eat breakfast, lunch, or dinner here since the market starts early at 7 a.m. and goes on until 10 p.m. With prices often running from $10 to $20 per dish, St. Roch

Market is a great place to enjoy a variety of foods without breaking the budget. The hall buzzes with the energy of children and families, residents and guests, all pulled in by the easygoing and pleasant environment. Outdoor sitting gives a view of the neighboring area, adding a bit of local color to the dinner experience. The choices at St. Roch Market are as varied as they are delicious, with each seller adding something unique to the table like cozy grilled cheese sandwiches and scrumptious Cuban samplers. Specialty meals like pho with roast beef, buns loaded with juicy chicken, and crisp fries with creamy white sauce showcase the market's original culinary style. St. Roch Market is also a great choice for groups, giving a variety of options that make it simple for everyone to pick something they'll enjoy.

- **Blue Cypress Books**

Blue Cypress Books is a famous small store, drawing book fans and travelers alike since 2008. Tucked away at *8123 Oak St, New Orleans, LA 70118*, this two-story store comes with a pleasant, homey vibe, where shelves fill with an eclectic mix of classic and modern literature, poetry, mystery, science fiction, art, and local works. Their well-curated collection includes a considerable number of old children's books, making it a wonderful place for families. Blue Cypress Books centers on community, encouraging customers to buy, sell, and share books while finding odd finds. The place is loaded with character, from a resident cat that roams the halls to the friendly staff who are glad to suggest new choices or help guests seek a beloved book. For those in search of a calm bookstore experience, Blue Cypress Books offers a great mix of range and mood.

With its cozy nooks and helpful attitude, it invites guests to sit, explore, and lose themselves in the pages of a new book. A loyalty card system lets readers earn points toward future purchases. Open daily from 10 a.m. to 6 p.m., Blue Cypress Books is also home to occasional events and literary meetings, supporting the unique culture of New Orleans.

- **Octavia Books**

Octavia Books is an appealing independent library located at *513 Octavia St, New Orleans, LA 70115*, presenting a lovingly chosen inventory that has made it a treasured location. Known for its vast layout and lovely atmosphere, Octavia Books encourages visitors to explore via its different rooms, each thoughtfully made to make looking simple and enjoyable. With categories like current fiction, non-fiction, a strong sci-fi and fantasy library, this store has something for every reading taste.

The cozy children's department is a beloved area for young readers and families, adding a pleasant touch to the shop's different choices. Staff members are polite, informed, and ready to serve, ensuring guests leave with a great book or a wonderful experience. The store's quiet patio area welcomes visitors to stay, giving a calm setting where book lovers can interact with the written word. Beyond its well-curated shelves, Octavia Books is a cornerstone for New Orleans' literary culture, regularly planning book signings, author talks, and community events that feature both local and national writers. These events build a feeling of community and allow fans to connect directly with writers, creating talks about new books and literary favorites. With its commitment to promoting small publishing and selected choices, Octavia Books offers a customized experience that feels new in today's fast-paced world. Open every day from 10 a.m., it's the ideal area to lose yourself in a good book, spend some peaceful time on the deck, or buy a unique present like bookmarks or tote bags.

- **Home Malone**

Home Malone located at *629 N Carrollton Ave, New Orleans, LA 70119,* offers a thorough journey into Southern creativity and workmanship, making it a remarkable location for individuals who adore backing local talent. Specializing in unique, handmade goods from small companies around the Deep South, this art and gift shop is loaded with bright, high-quality works by local artists. With an attractive selection of items, locally made jewelry, art to home décor and clothes, Home Malone

represents the beauty and creativity of New Orleans while being rooted in its community-oriented ideals. Every object sold has a story, an ode to the shop's commitment to boosting small, independent businesses, making an excellent setting for gift-buying or finding a memorable memory. Beyond merely a shopping experience, Home Malone also offers engaging classes and paint parties, where visitors get to join the creative process directly. These events give a fun chance to learn about the local art scene, create something beautiful, and connect with people in a relaxing environment. Located conveniently along N. Carrollton Ave., only a short train trip away, this hidden gem is easily approachable. The shop's surroundings, packed with the spirit of local art, add to its draw, giving each visit a real cultural experience.

- **Miette**

Miette is a secret paradise of fun, art, and unique gems that reflect the city's dynamic and quirky culture. Located at *2038 Magazine St, New Orleans,*

LA 70130, this shop captivates guests with a

carefully chosen mix of locally made jewelry, odd home decorations, interesting clothes, and even animal items. Comprising costume components, headdresses as well as carnival-inspired art, Miette is full of unique and creative treats at every step. Step inside and enjoy an interesting atmosphere where talent and imagination mix, making it easy to lose track of time while finding surprising gifts made by local artists. The shop's bright and friendly setting brilliantly depicts the spirit of New Orleans, mixing happy, lively items with more delicate and unique art forms.

Upstairs, Miette offers a more personal room devoted to adults, packed with body-positive art, odd pins, posters, and works that appeal to a sense of fun and celebration of uniqueness. This extra layer of finding makes Miette an experience where each visit seems like a short journey with something new to unearth every time. With the educated and polite staff excited about supporting local artists, buying here feels both personal and important.

SHOPPING AND SOUVENIRS

New Orleans is a treasure trove for shopping, offering a varied mix of gifts, old products, art, and locally made goods. With quirky shops, vintage stores and art galleries, there's no lack of amazing finds. Shoppers can discover items like handmade jewelry, home décor, old items and bright artwork that reflect the city's creative spirit:

- **Dirty Coast**

Dirty Coast at *1320 Magazine St Suite 105, New Orleans, LA 70130,* is a famous locally owned gift shop that has been a feature of New Orleans since 2005. Known for its funny and culturally rich t-shirt designs, the business offers a selection of entertaining, New Orleans-inspired products, including caps, socks, koozies, postcards, books, and kids' presents. The designs reflect the city's lively culture, its sense of humor, and its natural charm, making it a great place for getting an important or funny souvenir. With a concentration on expert, sometimes tongue-in-cheek connections, it's simple to locate anything that epitomizes the spirit of New Orleans. The shop's warm environment is matched by its nice and helpful staff, who go out of their way to make shopping here a lovely experience. Customers can expect an interesting shopping atmosphere, with professionals ready to help in finding the ideal present or perhaps a funny shirt that embodies the soul of New Orleans. Dirty Coast is the best spot to pick up locally made things that seem personal and real, offering crazy t-shirts and thoughtful Louisiana-themed gifts.

- **Fleurty Girl Magazine St.**

Fleurty Girl on Magazine Street is a must-visit spot for finding unique, New Orleans-inspired clothes, accessories, and gifts. This lively and friendly shop offers a lovely variety of regionally inspired t-shirts, elegant home décor, and odd gifts that perfectly reflect the spirit of the city. With eye-catching vinyl stickers, bright kitchen towels and customized goods, every piece reflects the charm and spirit of

New Orleans, making it an ideal stop for anyone looking to carry a bit of the city with them. The shop's nice and helpful staff add to the experience, always ready to assist with finding the ideal item, making personal suggestions, and ensuring that every visitor feels welcomed. The boutique's roomy and well-organized plan makes shopping simple and pleasurable, with a carefully chosen range of things for all ages and hobbies. If you're walking down Magazine Street, make sure to take a minute to visit Fleurty Girl—it's the ideal site for picking up one-of-a-kind presents or goodies for yourself, and it's a great alternative to the typical touristy gift shops.

- **Frenchmen Art Bazaar**

The Frenchmen Art Bazaar is a colorful, open-air market that offers an interesting and varied mix of local art, crafts, and strange items, making it a must-visit for experiencing the creative heart of New Orleans. Located at *619 Frenchmen St, New Orleans, LA 70116*, this market includes a broad selection of artwork by bright local artists, with paintings, prints, handmade jewelry and odd crafts.

It's a fantastic stop for getting unusual gifts or adding a bit of NOLA-inspired art to any collection. Open every evening from 7 pm, except Sundays, it's an excellent spot to explore as part of a night out. What makes the Frenchmen Art Bazaar so appealing is its laid-back and busy environment, where visitors can explore the artist booths while taking in the energy of Frenchmen Street's music culture.

The market continues to open late into the night, making it a great stop after experiencing the local nightlife. The warm glow of string lights, along with the lively throng, makes for a welcome and happy feeling. It's a nice departure from the normal bar scene and gives a chance to engage directly with the artists who are frequently present to talk about their work.

SEASONAL ACTIVITIES AND CELEBRATIONS

Spring: Blooms, Music, and Outdoor Fun

Spring in New Orleans is a lively season of rebirth when the city comes alive with a burst of color, music, and outdoor activities. As the weather starts to change and the city shakes off its winter cold, New Orleans presents a beautiful mix of blooming flowers, busy events, and open-air entertainment, making it the ideal time to explore and enjoy the city's unique draw. From the famous French Quarter to the beautiful grounds of the Garden District, the city becomes a tapestry of bright colors and numerous cultural activities. And springtime in New Orleans is a call to go outdoors, take in the city's liveliness, and enjoy the various sights, sounds, and tastes that characterize the season.

The beauty of New Orleans in April is best enjoyed via its amazing parks and flower displays. One of the city's most famous places to view spring growing is the New Orleans Botanical Garden, where thousands of flowers burst into color throughout its vast grounds. The beautiful gardens provide a calm escape from the busy streets, with scented roses, azaleas, and magnolias giving a magnificent background for a leisurely walk. For a more historical view of the city's growing season, the Garden District is a must-see. The tree-lined streets are covered by giant oaks, while grand houses with their colorful front yards and gardens bloom with azaleas and camellias. If you're in the mood for a more full experience, the annual "Festival of Flowers" at the Longue Vue House and Gardens shows a spectacular assortment of local flora, where you can learn about the region's distinctive plant life and even take home gardening ideas.

Spring also brings about more music, as the city's famous jazz and blues culture hits its height. New Orleans comes alive with festivals, bands, and street performers, making it the perfect time to enjoy the city's rich musical culture. The famous French Quarter has several outdoor music events, where the sounds of jazz and brass bands flow into the streets, bringing crowds to dance, cheer, and sing along. The French Quarter Festival, normally held in April, is one of the city's most famous events, bringing together local artists for a weekend of free music, food, and fun in the center of the city. This event features dozens of stages spread around the Quarter, and it's a celebration of everything that makes New Orleans unique; live music, delicious food, and the happy energy of the city. If you want something a little more personal, try out the Spotted Cat Music Club on Frenchmen Street, where you can hear true New Orleans jazz in a tiny, no-frills setting.

Spring in New Orleans is also about enjoying the outdoors. With the weather being just right, the city's various parks, riversides, and bike paths give plenty of area for outdoor fun. City Park, one of the biggest urban parks in the nation, becomes a hive of activity throughout spring. Visitors can hire a pedal boat and cruise across the gorgeous Big Lake, take a relaxed bike ride along the park's numerous beautiful walks, or eat in one of its many open spots. The park's Sculpture Garden is especially beautiful in spring when the flowers and trees are in full bloom, giving a friendly setting for art fans and nature lovers alike. For those hoping to enjoy the Mississippi River, take a barge trip to view the city from a fresh viewpoint. The natural beauty mixed with the river's prominent sites gives an amazing outdoor trip. If you're wanting more exciting spring activities, the Audubon Zoo and Audubon Park give great chances for exploration and rest. Spring is the best season to visit the zoo, since the animals are more busy, and the weather makes walking among the exhibits nice.

You can even take a spin on the old wheel or have lunch at one of the zoo's picnic places. Audubon Park, with its huge green fields and lovely oak trees, is also an excellent place for a jog, a relaxing walk, and a game of frisbee with friends. Another odd spring activity is to visit the Treme area during the famous second-line parades. These unplanned, energetic street parties are filled with colorful costumes, brass bands, and exuberant dancing, usually occurring on weekends throughout spring, and provide a real experience of New Orleans' joyful atmosphere. For those interested in cultural events, spring is also the season for some of the city's most famous gatherings. The New Orleans

Jazz & tradition Festival, or Jazz Fest, is a highlight of the spring, bringing people from across the world to enjoy the city's rich musical tradition. Held in late April or early May, Jazz Fest includes a range of world-class singers, with classic jazz artists and current acts, all playing at the Fair Grounds Race Course. Along with music, the event also offers local food booths offering traditional New Orleans treats such as jambalaya, crawfish étouffée, and po'boys. It's a real celebration of the city's culture, and no visit to New Orleans in spring is complete without watching this famous event.

Summer: Beating the Heat with Indoor Escapes

New Orleans summers can be hot, but there's no reason to let the heat keep you from experiencing all the rich culture, history, and art the city has to offer. Luckily, New Orleans is filled with indoor getaways that give a nice break from the heat while still allowing you to experience the heart and spirit of the city.

For art enthusiasts, the New Orleans Museum of Art (NOMA) is a great spot. Located in the green City Park, this museum displays an amazing collection of over 40,000 pieces of art, covering times and countries. Showcasing old European works and modern art, NOMA's halls provide a cool and quiet refuge from the summer heat. The museum is also home to the Besthoff Sculpture Garden, an outdoor paradise of large-scale statues, but even the inside halls provide a peaceful experience with their climate-controlled settings.

History fans can dive into New Orleans' rich past with a visit to the National WWII Museum, one of the most known museums in the country. It's not only for history fans, its engaging shows and detailed displays make it a must-see for all visitors. The museum is huge and air-conditioned, perfect for escaping the heat while learning about the massive effect of globe War II on the globe.

- **Louisiana State Museum**

The Louisiana State Museum is another great stop for history buffs, with a range of shows linked to the state's history, culture, and unique customs. Located at *751 Chartres St, New Orleans, LA 70116,* this museum offers an entertaining trip through the state's unique and difficult past. Open from 9 AM to 4 PM, with a shutdown on Mondays, this museum gives guests two levels of interesting displays. The first floor is given to Hurricane Katrina, one of the most important events in the city's modern past. Through stunning exhibits and unique items, the show explores the tale of the storm's damage, its impact on New Orleans, and the tenacity of the community that has rebuilt itself in the years afterward. It gives a deep, emotional look into the tragedy and its effects, showing both the battles and the successes of the individuals touched by the disaster. On the second floor, the tone changes as guests dig into the bright and joyful past of Mardi Gras. The displays demonstrate the customs, pomp, and culture surrounding this famous holiday. With the bright outfits, masks, the history of the parades and the importance of king cakes and beads, the Mardi Gras show gives a full look at the festival's cultural effect on Louisiana. Interactive displays and video shows bring the happy mood of the holiday to life, making it a joyful and instructive experience for all ages. Together, the museum's collection finds a balance between the sad memories of the past and the lively atmosphere of New Orleans.

- **The Cabildo**

The Cabildo, a historic 1790s structure located at *701 Chartres St, New Orleans, LA 70130*, is a must-visit spot for anybody interested in New

Orleans' rich and difficult past. Once the center of Spanish imperial power, it is now home to a fascinating museum that traces the city's history from its birth. The museum is open daily from 9 AM to 4 PM, but closed on Mondays. As visitors pass through its great doors, they are whisked through an interesting tale that covers many ages. On the ground floor, the focus is on the lively past of New Orleans, showing things from all across the city. The collection includes everyday things, gems that represent the cultural, political, and economic growth of this unique location.

The second floor of The Cabildo introduces guests further into the major times of New Orleans' history, especially the Battle of New Orleans and the effects of the Louisiana Purchase. This museum tells the Battle of 1815, which was fought near the city and sealed Andrew Jackson's place in American history. The show gives a full look into the fight and its fallout, helping to understand why Jackson's statue is such a famous sign in Jackson

Square. Additionally, the museum digs into the larger background of the Louisiana Purchase that was signed in The Cabildo's old parliamentary halls and grew the United States' area significantly. A visit to The Cabildo is a satisfying experience for history buffs and casual tourists alike, giving a rich, informative experience with amazing views of the square, and even a chance to take pictures from the windows of this architectural gem. The entry is fairly priced, making it a great chance to connect with New Orleans' past while soaking oneself in the beauty of the old building.

- **The Presbytère**

The Presbytère at *751 Chartres St, New Orleans, LA 70116,* is a famous building originally finished in 1813, and is a historic monument that has served numerous roles over its long history, such as a religious house and a courthouse, until it was turned into a museum. Now a part of the Louisiana State Museum, the Presbytère presents an interesting study of two of the most important events in the city's history. For approximately $7 per person, visitors can get insight into the damage caused by Hurricane Katrina on the first story and the lively celebration of Mardi Gras on the second floor. With a budget friendly ticket price, the museum gives good value, particularly for visitors seeking relief from the heat, since the cool interior also offers spectacular views of Jackson Square. The storm show on the first floor is especially touching, focusing on the effect of the disaster and the problems faced by the city in its wake. Detailed displays on levees, water management, and the efforts to rebuild New Orleans show the resilience of the city and its people.

On the second floor, the Mardi Gras show dazzles with its bright display of costumes, history, and cultural importance. This part gives a thorough dive into the beginnings of the holiday, from its start on Epiphany (January 6th) to its spectacular conclusion on Fat Tuesday before Lent. Visitors will admire the beautiful outfits and magnificent jewels made for the queens of Mardi Gras, as well as learn about the traditions, krewes, and famous themes that make the parade season so special to New

Orleans. The Presbytère wonderfully depicts the atmosphere of New Orleans, mixing the sadness of Hurricane Katrina with the joyous and exuberant celebration of Mardi Gras. It's a fantastic spot to immerse oneself in the city's complicated past while having a cool and quiet break from the busy streets outside.

- **Canal Place**

For experiencing a more laid-back holiday, The Shops at Canal Place offer high-end shopping in a nice, air-conditioned setting. It is a famous shopping location that improves the buying experience in the center of New Orleans. Spanning three elegant floors, this high-end shopping complex located at *333 Canal St, New Orleans, LA 70130,* offers a chosen collection of brand-name businesses that appeal to fashion fans, trendsetters, and those wanting beautiful items. Luxury brands like Saks Fifth Avenue, Louis Vuitton, and Tiffany & Co. are featured alongside modern favorites such as Lululemon and Anthropologie, promising there's something for every taste. And whatever it is you seek, Canal Place offers a posh and pleasant atmosphere to shop the greatest collections from around the globe. The wide layout, paired with fantastic air conditioning, makes it a tempting haven even on the hottest New Orleans days. Beyond shopping, Canal Place also offers lots of chances to relax. The Westin Hotel, which is joined by the mall, includes a public bar and lounge with amazing views, great for relaxing after a day of shopping or visiting. For those looking for a little fun, the mall offers a huge food area and a movie theater, giving extra choices for a well-rounded visit.

For those who wish to enjoy New Orleans' jazz culture in a small setting, The Spotted Cat Music Club creates the perfect atmosphere with a cool setting perfect for enjoying the exciting sounds of New Orleans jazz. Another great indoor escape is The Audubon Aquarium of the Americas, located along the Mississippi Riverfront. This beautiful institution provides a full experience with displays dedicated to the sea life of the Gulf of Mexico and beyond.

- **Escape My Room New Orleans**

For something a little more involved and enjoyable, you can check out the Escape My Room experience, an exciting puzzle-solving exercise where teams of friends or family members work together to escape from a series of themed rooms. Escape My Room New Orleans offers a truly engaging and active mystery-solving experience, appropriate for an exciting and unique adventure. Located at *1152 Camp St, New Orleans, LA 70130,* in a beautiful old structure that oozes an Old South ambiance, the facility features themed escape rooms that take guests into a world of tension, drama, and mystery.

Here, visitors will quickly be drawn into the mood, with the surroundings thoughtfully arranged to reflect the idea of each room. The cells are less about locks and passwords and more focused on puzzles and reading, putting a new twist on the standard escape room format. What makes Escape

My Room New Orleans unique is its interactive element. Each event is led by a speaker who plays an important part in the tale, giving a layer of performance that connects guests on a deeper level. This engaging touch makes the game seem more like a live dramatic show, where you're not simply solving tasks but actively engaging in a story. The whole journey takes place in a wonderful old building, further adding to the mood. With polite and knowledgeable guides, each room has tasks that are both entertaining and satisfying, making it a fantastic activity for families, friends, or anybody hoping to dive into New Orleans' mysterious side.

Fall: Halloween Parades and Haunted Tours

When fall comes in New Orleans, the city turns into a fascinating mixture of scary stories, exuberant events, and spooky experiences that reflect its rich history and colorful culture. The brisk fall air, mixed with the appeal of the Halloween season, pulls all to experience the scary side of this old city. Halloween in New Orleans is a time for thrilling parades, eerie tours, and engaging experiences that are particularly linked to the city's spirit of mystery and old-world charm.

One of the most exciting ways to enjoy Halloween in New Orleans is by joining one of its famous Halloween parades. The most famous of them is the Krewe of Boo, New Orleans' official Halloween parade that takes place each year on the weekend before Halloween. This bright parade goes through the French Quarter, with float riders dressed in spectacular outfits, tossing beads and other gifts to the onlookers. The parade is a celebration of both New Orleans' rich racial past and the spooky mood of Halloween. The Krewe of Boo is famous for its bright and colorful floats, many of which have a dark or spooky theme. Expect to witness witches, vampires, and monsters from your worst fears make their way through the streets, all supported by marching bands, dancers, and performers that create an atmosphere full of joy and fear. Adding to the Krewe of Boo, New Orleans performs several smaller parades and neighborhood events that honor the Halloween spirit. These events frequently combine costume battles, live music, and dance acts, bringing forth the best of New Orleans' rich culture while enjoying the funny, scary side of the season.

For those looking for something more personal and themed, the Frenchmen Street neighborhood comes alive with scary events in its bars and clubs, where you can enjoy live jazz with a macabre touch. From the exciting party scene in the Marigny to the historical center of the French Quarter, Halloween in New Orleans offers a broad choice of parades, events, and activities for everyone, no matter their age or hobbies. For a more spine-chilling experience, ghost walks are an important element of Halloween parties. New Orleans is famous for its spooky history, and there's no better time to dig into its scary past than during the autumn. Ghost tours are an essential must, with several conducting midnight trips through the gloomy streets of the French Quarter, where you'll hear stories of restless spirits, cursed locations, and the terrible events that have formed the city's haunting reputation.

- **Ghost City Tours in New Orleans**

The most popular ghost outings, such as The Ghosts of the French Quarter Tour, sometimes include stops at haunted hotels, houses, and graveyards, where guides relate scary tales about the ghosts that are supposed to still stay. Ghost City Tours in New Orleans is one of the most interesting and entertaining ways to explore the ghostly past of the French Quarter. With a range of adventures designed to suit all sorts of guests. Each tour is given by skilled experts who are excited about New Orleans' eerie legend, presenting an educational and interesting mixture of scary tales and historical insights. Rates for these trips start at $25 per person, giving an economical chance to dive into the city's scary past. The tours are famed for their distinctive storytelling, with guides cleverly mixing scary ghost tales with rich historical insights. Visitors are attracted by the fascinating stories that develop as they stroll through the ancient streets, from the terrible past of haunted buildings to the restless ghosts claiming to still prowl the neighborhood. For those wanting an exciting yet family-friendly experience, Ghost City offers tours that are both instructive and fun, with a great mix of scary and educational material. For a more adult-only experience, their ghost bar walk allows customers to have a drink while learning about the strange past of New Orleans' drinking places. Regardless of the tour you pick, the mix of Southern charm, scary stories, and historic drama offers a fascinating experience that is excellent for anyone hoping to add a little fear to their New Orleans holiday.

For a more thorough experience, take a voodoo trip, where you'll learn about the mysterious side of New Orleans, including the customs of voodoo queens like Marie Laveau. The trip will take you to major places connected to voodoo and the city's interesting, often dark, link with the supernatural. You'll learn how New Orleans' voodoo traditions have been woven into its cultural fabric, with an investigation of the customs, beliefs, and spiritual practices that have inspired not just the city's history but also its Halloween festivities.

For Something new, take a cemetery trip that sees the above-ground graves in New Orleans' famous cemeteries. The city's above-ground burying custom, inspired by its swampy land, gives the cemetery a distinctively scary aspect, and many trips dive into the lore surrounding the individuals buried there. One of the most notable places is St. Louis Cemetery No. 1, home to the grave of Marie Laveau, where guests can learn about her effect on both voodoo practices and the city's spiritual customs. It's a chance to connect with New Orleans' rich cultural history and its interesting ideas about life, death, and the supernatural.

Winter: Christmas and New Year's Fireworks

New Orleans is a city known for its bright spirit and festive energy, and when winter comes around, the events only get more magnificent, with Christmas and New Year's fireworks lighting up the sky. The holidays in the Big Easy are a unique mix of national customs, music, and, of course, stunning fireworks shows that honor both Christmas and New Year's Eve in the most memorable fashion. As the season's frost sinks in, the crisp air is filled with the excitement of expectation as the city prepares for its famous Christmas events and enjoying the beauty of New Orleans' Christmas lights is an experience that epitomizes the kindness and charm of the city throughout the winter season.

On Christmas Eve, the sky above the Mississippi River comes alive with a breathtaking display of fireworks, usually followed by a joyful party along the riverbanks. The yearly fireworks show, seen from areas such as Woldenberg Park and the French Quarter, is a highlight of the season, celebrating the holiday in spectacular form.

Woldenberg Park is a calm refuge directly on the Mississippi River, giving a wonderful escape from the rush and bustle of the French Quarter. This 16-acre waterfront park is a favorite draw with sufficient green space, running lanes, and beautiful views of the river and the Algiers Point neighborhood. Open daily from 6 a.m., Woldenberg Park is great for enjoying a leisurely walk, lunch by the lake, resting and watching the boats glide by.

With free entry, the park's beautiful draw is complemented by statues, sculptures, and tiny ponds dotted throughout, giving it a peaceful atmosphere to take in the views of the Mississippi River and the ships going by. Its central position, close to sights like the Aquarium of the Americas and the Algiers Ferry, gives it a great starting place for further exploring the city. Woldenberg Park is also a family-friendly site with lots of services for all ages. The park includes easy walking paths, seats, and vast open areas, great for a peaceful day with loved ones. The park's closeness to the French Quarter makes it a handy stop before continuing to other sites, or it may serve as a calm break after a day of touring. With well-maintained bathroom facilities and adequate areas for kids to play, it's a great spot for a short stop or an extended stay. For those hoping to enjoy the riverside, the nearby dike offers a nice area to walk along the water, and the stunning views of downtown New Orleans and the Algiers Point neighborhood make a beautiful background for a calm day outside.

Families, friends, and couples gather on the riverbank, warmed up in the winter weather, to watch as the sky explodes into color, dazzling the skyline and reflecting off the river's surface. This lovely moment is accentuated by the sound of Christmas music moving through the air, while live shows and activities add to the holiday mood of the night. However, it's on New Year's Eve when the fireworks take center stage in New Orleans. The city's famous New Year's Eve fireworks show is a sight unlike any other, as the countdown to midnight is marked by bright blasts of color and light that fill the night sky. A favorite spot to ring in the new year is Jackson Square, where throngs gather to see the fireworks light up the skyline and the Mississippi River. The music of the fireworks mingles with the lively beats of jazz, creating a joyous mood that is both joyful and magnificent. As midnight approaches, the whole city is aglow, with people sharing New Year's wishes beneath the magnificent bursts of color, while the ancient buildings of the French Quarter and the river offer the ideal setting for the party.

The city's New Year's Eve fireworks are even more beautiful when watched from a river tour, where you can enjoy the show from the water, adding an added element of beauty and elegance to the evening. Several firms offer fireworks boats along the Mississippi River, giving a front-row experience to the bright show. The fireworks reflect on the lake, creating a mirror picture of the sky's spectacular booms. New Orleans' New Year's Eve fireworks also weave into the unique culture of the city, mixing the custom of fireworks with the city's particular music scene. With jazz bands playing on the streets along with the brass bands sending the parties into the new year, the city's beat and energy are as much a part of the party as the fireworks themselves. The mix of sights and sounds creates a party that is truly New Orleans, giving you a once-in-a-lifetime chance to enjoy the holidays in a way that only this city can deliver.

ESSENTIAL TIPS FOR TRAVELERS

Navigating New Orleans' Public Transportation

New Orleans has various accessible public transit options to let you tour the city with ease, therefore understanding the city's public transportation system will promise that you make the most of your time while visiting New Orleans in a way that is both affordable and efficient.

One of the most lovely and known types of public transportation is the antique streetcar system. These antique cars have been a part of the city's beauty for over a century, giving a lovely and relaxing way to ride among the areas. The St. Charles Streetcar is the most famous line, carrying passengers from the Central Business District through the beautiful Garden District and uptown. The trip is a great chance to experience the beautiful architecture, lush gardens, and distinctive oak-lined streets of New Orleans while making your way to places like Audubon Park and the Garden

District. Another famous route is the Canal Streetcar that links the French Quarter to other regions of the city, including the Cemeteries and City Park, home to the New Orleans Museum of Art and the Botanic Gardens. Streetcar costs are reasonable, with day passes available for visitors wishing to jump on and off at their leisure.

For a more open method to get about, trains and buses are another trustworthy option. The bus system runs on the most important roads, linking places from downtown to the edges of the city. It's an easy method to go to places that aren't instantly covered by the train system. Buses are usually safe, but it's best to check routes and schedules ahead of time, since service may be less common during off-peak hours or on weekends. Like the streetcars, buses accept a range of price options, including pay-per-ride tickets and multi-day passes, so you can simply plan your trip according to your schedule.

For a unique and beautiful experience, boats are another must-try type of public transportation. The Algiers Ferry, which spans the Mississippi River from the French Quarter to Algiers Point, is an easy and fun trip that gives spectacular views of the river and the city skyline. It's a great chance to view New Orleans from the river while visiting the historic Algiers area, which has its charm, with busy local cafés, shops, and stores. The boat journey is short, but it's a fun and affordable way to visit the city's waterfront and find another side of New Orleans.

New Orleans is also becoming more bike-friendly, with bike-sharing programs like Blue Bikes New Orleans giving a handy and eco-friendly way to move about the city. These bikes are available at numerous sites across the city, and the method makes it simple to pick up and drop off bikes at different places. For those who desire a more private experience, walking might be one of the most fun ways to see the French Quarter and neighboring areas. Many of the city's most famous landmarks, from Jackson Square to the colorful streets of the Marigny and Faubourg Tremé, are best experienced on foot, as you can take in the sights, sounds, and smells of the city up close.

While New Orleans' public transport system is fairly simple to handle, it's crucial to plan, more so during busy tourist seasons when specific lines can get crowded or less regular. It's also worth noting that some places, especially in the areas, may not be as well-served by public transportation, so having a ride-sharing service like Uber or Lyft close might be important for those times when you require a more direct route. The good news is that New Orleans is a walkable city, and many of the best sites are located in areas where walking, biking, or utilizing the train is more than adequate to get about.

Important Emergency Contacts and Information

While visiting, it will be useful to have emergency contacts on hand for fast entry;

- In case of any pressing situation, calling 911 links you to local police, fire, and medical help.

- The New Orleans Police Agency (NOPD), can be reached for non-emergency problems at (504) 821-2222.

- For urgent medical needs, University Medical Center New Orleans is a vital hospital located in the city and is prepared to handle emergencies. Their main contact number is (504) 702-3000.

- Another close hospital is Tulane Medical Center, available at (504) 988-5263. For poison-related help, the Louisiana Poison

Control Center can be reached at 1-800-222-1222.

- For visitors that require help, New Orleans Visitor Information Services gives support and can be contacted at (504) 566-5011. They also give local help if you face any issues throughout your stay.

- Most importantly, stay current with weather reports, especially during storm season, via the National Weather Service by visiting weather.gov or checking into local programs.

Apps and Websites to Make Your Stay Smoother

New Orleans boasts a rich mix of culture, history, and entertainment, and utilizing the proper apps and websites will improve your experience by giving quick entry to everything the city offers.

- **NOLA Ready** is an important tool, especially during storm season. It provides real-time emergency alerts, road bans, and details on city events.

- For moving about, **RTA GoMobile** is important for public transport, allowing you to buy bus and subway tickets, check routes, and access times to make traveling the city easier.

- For keeping an eye on food and leisure, **Yelp** and **OpenTable** make it simple to find famous places, check reviews, and even book seats, which is beneficial for high-demand areas.

- For local events, **WWOZ 90.7 FM's** website and app provide a list of live music, which is a vital component of the New Orleans experience.

- **Eventbrite** regularly features interesting pop-ups, events, and parades throughout the city.

- For outings, **Ghost City trips** and **Viator** are fantastic for booking unique local experiences, like ghost tours and historical walks.

FINAL WORDS

As your trip through New Orleans draws to a close, it's clear that this city leaves its mark. New Orleans has a way of making all feel both energized and emotionally linked. Every neighborhood, every taste, and every tale adds to its fabric, giving you experiences and memories that will last long after you've gone. In hopes that this guide has helped you experience the many sights, sounds, and tastes of the city with ease and excitement. In a city where history meets the present in dynamic ways, and where each corner offers something surprising, New Orleans is an experience in learning the art of living completely. Here's to accepting the spirit of this great city and to bringing a part of its charm with you, wherever you go next. Safe travels, and may New Orleans always seem like a second home.

Made in the USA
Columbia, SC
07 December 2024

48686317R00078